"We are all called to holiness. Yet finding our way to sanctity through the maze of the consumerism and secularism of our age is not always easy. Kevin Lowry's *Faith at Work* sheds great light on the pathway to a genuine life in the Spirit. This insightful and engaging book offers practical guidance to transforming the routine of everyday work into a life-giving participation in bearing witness to the Gospel and our own share in manifesting Christ's kingdom. This book helps us capture the joy of seeing the wonder of God at work all around us in the very things we do — how we live."

CARDINAL DONALD WUERL, archbishop of Washington

"Kevin's book is an important reminder that we are called to live our faith in our work, where we spend so much of our life. He offers wonderful insights centered on serving others but does so by revealing an unwavering commitment towards keeping Christ at the top of one's priorities, regardless of the demands of the workplace. The recommendations and questions for reflection at the end of each chapter offer simple steps on how to put this book into action."

J. DAVID KARAM, president, Wendy's International, Inc.

"In our society, faith and work are often presented as things that don't mix or shouldn't be mixed; yet nothing could be further from the truth. In this book, Kevin skillfully shows how we are in fact called to sanctity in and through our work. *Faith at Work* is both practical and inspiring!"

TOM MONAGHAN, founder,
Domino's Pizza, Inc., and Ave Maria University

"Too many Christians treat 'ambition' and 'success' as if they're four-letter words. They're not. For a Catholic in business, they can be touchstones of sanctification. Kevin Lowry knows that, and he shows us how to turn a career of nine-to-five into a lasting encounter with Jesus Christ."

SCOTT _____, _____, _____ of Biblical Theology,
_____teubenville

"In today's struggling economy, many people are grateful simply to be on someone's payroll. But as Kevin so eloquently explains in *Faith at Work*, our jobs, no matter how big or small, can serve as a mission field where we can help others and ourselves achieve that universal call to holiness. Kevin provides us with plenty of career common sense, drawing from his own workplace experience combined with sound Catholic teaching. This book will help many people be the best they can be."

TERESA TOMEO,
syndicated Catholic talk show host, best-selling
Catholic author, and motivational speaker

"What if your job was not *just* a job? What if your work was actually central to your faith? In *Faith at Work*, Kevin Lowry shows how Christians can bring their faith to the world of cubicles, emails, bosses, and factories. Through personal examples, stories of success, and biblical guidelines, Kevin paves the way toward a 'spirituality of work.' If you work — and who doesn't?! — this book will help you tremendously."

BRANDON VOGT,
Catholic blogger and author of *The Church and New Media*

"Kevin Lowry writes in a very easy-to-read style, but don't take that to mean this book is fluff. It is anything but. This book is filled with advice, wisdom, and Scripture that will help anyone in the workplace — and beyond — become a saint. As Kevin says, all of us are on 'a mission from God,' and that mission, filled with adventure and challenge, will take us right back to God if we do His will in every aspect of our lives. This book will help."

RACHEL MUHA,
The Brian Muha Memorial Foundation, Inc.,
The Run the Race Club

"In an age when workplaces, office hours, and business ethics are being redefined, Kevin Lowry's new book *Faith at Work* is an essential resource for anyone engaged in work, whether the reader is a seasoned professional or a brand-new recruit. With an emphasis on both spiritual exercises and professional pointers to help you succeed at both your career and at life, *Faith at Work* provides a hallmark for personal excellence. Inspirational, well-written, and full of insight, Kevin Lowry's *Faith at Work* provides the motivation, the means, and the message needed for anyone looking to make a true difference in our world."

LISA M. HENDEY,
founder and editor of www.CatholicMom.com
and author of *A Book of Saints for Catholic Moms*

"*Faith at Work* is a source of both encouragement and challenge. We know that by living Christian virtues in the workplace, an opportunity exists for the Holy Spirit to work in the hearts of those whose lives we touch. The challenge is remaining true to our baptisms and allowing God's power to permeate us in every role we play. As a longtime friend, adviser, and now colleague, I know Kevin strives to practice what he preaches in this book. Catholics, and all Christians, will benefit from reading this book and reflecting on the lessons of the Gospel applied to our everyday work."

MARCUS GRODI,
president and founder,
The Coming Home Network International

"I can't imagine any person, no matter the job title, who would not find *Faith at Work* to be both practical and inspiring. Too many people compartmentalize their faith and their work, thinking that it is impossible to bring faith into the workplace. Kevin Lowry demonstrates, with simple and relatable examples and suggestions, just how wrong that is! The book is filled with simple, yet profound and challenging advice. Among my favorites: 'Recognize the difference between serving and making people happy'; 'Jesus loved everyone He met, and He demonstrated this love through friendship. The workplace affords us an outstanding opportunity to be friends to others'; 'When we enter the workplace, we aren't always in a position to quote Bible verses, or to illustrate our points with citations from encyclicals. But we're always able to conduct ourselves with virtue and honor.'

"If every reader put only one of Kevin's suggestions into practice on a regular basis, workplaces — and lives — would be changed, through God's grace."

PEGGY HARTSHORN, PH.D.,
president, Heartbeat International

"Are you concerned about the direction of your own career; about setting priorities and balancing commitments to your family, your career, and to God; about how to cope with a difficult coworker; about how to spread the Gospel and share simple Christian love within the workplace, inspiring, and not repelling, others? Kevin Lowry wrote *Faith at Work* to help us allow our faith to lead our career efforts and to address these issues and more. Judging from the results, I pray that Kevin's own career efforts will include writing many more books!

"*Faith at Work* is suffused with the spirit of charity; with warm, good-hearted humor; and with hard-won practical wisdom wrung from decades of real-life experience in the work world. This is one of those books I'll pull out from time to time and read again and again with relish, until, and perhaps even after, the day that I retire. I'll be putting copies in the hands of my two sons as well. In the meanwhile, I can hardly wait to get back to the office to put *Faith at Work* to work at work!"

KEVIN VOST, PSY.D.,
author of *Memorize the Faith!*
and *From Atheism to Catholicism*

"Kevin Lowry's *Faith at Work* is a gift to Catholics everywhere. All of us have a job to do, whether it's as a corporate executive or as a stay-at-home mom. My own career path has taken many turns, from scooping ice cream in high school to managing a ten-million-dollar payroll to changing diapers. At every turn, seeking God in my work was vital, not only in helping me do my job well but also for my eternal soul.

"*Faith at Work* will help you ease work-related stress, deal effectively with office politics, find fulfillment in your job, and most importantly, grow in faith through your work."

MAUREEN WITTMANN,
author and co-founder of Homeschool Connections

"I've known Kevin Lowry as a Catholic and a businessman for the better part of two decades. And I've been waiting all that time for him to write THE book on faith in the workplace. Reading this book is a privilege — like the chance to learn shortstop from Derek Jeter or songwriting from Paul McCartney. Take notes."

MIKE AQUILINA,
author and executive vice president
of the St. Paul Center for Biblical Theology

"At the heart of the pontificates of Blessed John Paul II and Pope Benedict XVI is a proper explanation and putting into action of the core message of the Second Vatican Council, which is 'The Universal Call to Holiness,' and that includes the 98.5 percent of the faithful of the Church who are lay people. Only if they are energized and helped to seek and live holiness in the middle of the world can the 'new springtime' of the Church be accomplished. In this fine, readable, and eminently practical book, Kevin Lowry shows in this case 'the angel is in the practical details.' This 'how to' book will help you to imitate Jesus in His hidden life as a working person and to live day by day what Blessed John Paul II referred to as the 'Fifth Gospel.'"

FATHER C. JOHN McCLOSKEY,
Church historian and research fellow at the
Faith and Reason Institute in Washington, DC

"Kevin writes in a clear and concise manner, using a conversational tone and pertinent stories to share timeless lessons and eternal truths.

Each chapter features easy-to-understand-and-implement 'action items' for the journey. *Faith at Work* is inspired and will prove to be a true blessing to its readers and their colleagues."

TOM PETERSON,
founder and president,
Catholics Come Home.org ®

"A concise, helpful tool for the faith-full working man or woman in a culture and business world that often encourages anything but faith-fullness."

ALLEN HUNT, PH.D.,
author of *Confessions of a Mega-Church Pastor: How I Discovered the Hidden Treasures of the Catholic Church*

"Kevin offers the reader practical insights from his experiences in life that will inspire you to bring Christ into your workplace and family. You'll see the workplace as an opportunity to usher in His Kingdom."

KATIE GESTO,
lay missionary, Sudan

"We Catholics are notoriously weak in witnessing to our faith. As an enthusiastic, well-informed convert, Mr. Lowry unerringly guides us into the 1-2-3's of 'letting our lights shine' for Christ. This book is clearly written, eminently practical in its advice. All of us can profit greatly from reading it and putting it into practice."

FATHER RAY RYLAND,
former Episcopalian, author, and columnist for
The Catholic Answer magazine

Faith
at
Work

Faith
at
Work

Finding Purpose
Beyond the Paycheck

Kevin Lowry

Our Sunday Visitor Publishing Division
Our Sunday Visitor, Inc.
Huntington, Indiana 46750

ISBN: 978-1-59276-016-9 (Inventory No. T1178)
eISBN: 978-1-61278-134-1
LCCN: 2011939336

Cover design: Lindsey Riesen
Cover image: Shutterstock and The Crosiers
Interior design: Sherri L. Hoffman
Interior art: iStockphoto

PRINTED IN THE UNITED STATES OF AMERICA

Dedicated to my beloved wife, Kathi, the crown jewel of my life, and the supreme gifts of our marriage: Christian, T.J., Sarah, Daniel, Maria, Joseph, David, and Hannah.

Kathi, our children are beautiful — I love you!

Contents

Foreword

We Americans didn't start the Industrial Revolution. We just powered it with a steam engine. Then, for two centuries, we rolled up our sleeves and put Western civilization on an assembly line. The results have been pretty spectacular: antibiotics, automobiles, refrigerators, electric lights, long-life expectancy, etc.

It's not so many generations since Benjamin Franklin turned cranks to run his muscle-powered mechanical printing presses. Now we can travel with more books stored in our telephones than the ancient Egyptians kept in their vast library at Alexandria.

We have invented all this and so much more. We've also given the world the midlife crisis, the life coach, and the concept of a career — and a second career. We didn't create discontent, of course. We just powered it with a steam engine.

Kevin Lowry is a seasoned accountant and a business executive, so he knows all about the many ways we can gain efficiency and productivity. But Kevin's also a Christian who prays, and so he hears a haunting question echo down the centuries: "What profit would there be for one to gain the whole world and forfeit his life? Or what can one give in exchange for his life?" (Matthew 16:26).

Perhaps the American thing to do, right now, would be to launch a fire-and-brimstone sermon about making an idol of work and so earning damnation after death. But there are more efficient ways to forfeit one's life. In fact, it's become fairly common to advance such misery from end-of-life to midlife. It's so common it's become a cliché: the story of the upwardly mobile professional who seems to have it all, but finds life utterly empty.

The greatest thinkers, from Augustine to Pascal to Springsteen, have concluded wisely that everybody has a hungry heart, a restless heart, an unfathomable heart. Your heart, like mine, can never be filled by the money we throw into it, no matter how much. It will not find rest in the largest mansion, no matter how big the pool.

The hole in our hearts is the size and shape, not of a sports car, but of God Himself. God Himself wants to fill our lives so that they'll never be empty. But He won't force us to be happy. It's amazing, but not even God can do that.

No matter how old we are, we cannot afford to delay. It's imperative that we draw closer to our Lord God now, and not tomorrow or next year. If we're not drawing closer, we're sliding away from happiness, meaning, and true success.

I'm reminded of a line from St. Thérèse of Lisieux: "We are living now in an age of inventions, and we no longer have to take the trouble of climbing stairs, for in the homes of the rich, an elevator has replaced these very successfully. I wanted to find an elevator which would raise me to Jesus, for I am too small to climb the rough stairway to perfection."

Thanks to Kevin Lowry, you have the technology. It's this book. A good businessman, Kevin has prepared for us a productive, efficient way to a profound supernatural life. I'll see you on the elevator, going up.

MIKE AQUILINA
Author and Executive Vice President of
the St. Paul Center for Biblical Theology

Why Write a Book About Work?

The only thing that matters is your conversion. In the end, we're all going to wind up in a box, several feet underground — but where will you spend eternity?

My goal in writing this book is to encourage you along the path of conversion. Whether you are a CEO, a homemaker, a clerk, a teacher, or a laborer, I want you to think about your work just a little bit differently. Work is an opportunity, not only to earn a living but also to live your faith in its fullness. The only way this is possible is to completely integrate your faith and your work.

We all have people in our lives that we love. In my case, my wife, Kathi, and our eight children are high on my list. There have been many times I have wanted to provide my kids with a legacy that goes beyond the flawed genetic material they received from me. Ever since they were little, I've told them I don't care about *what* they are when they grow up; I care about *who* they are. (In fairness, and in a spirit of full disclosure, I also told them that they need to make enough money to move out of the house.)

What I really want to impress upon them, though, is the importance of following God in every aspect of their lives, including their work. It doesn't matter whether they are chief executives of large corporations or sanitation engineers. There are many worthy pursuits that provide a paycheck. The point is that they need to think of work as central to their Christian vocations.

There is really no magic to integrating faith and work; it's more a process of faithfulness formed in the crucible of life, one day at a time. So next time you're at work (or anywhere else, for that matter) and feel like chucking it all, just remember to keep your gaze fixed on Christ, who encourages us to live a life of holiness, and who even gives us the tools to make it possible.

Acknowledgments

Writing this book has been a joy and a privilege. Like most worthwhile endeavors, there were many people involved who helped bring the project to fruition. I would like to thank my wife, Kathi, for her loving encouragement and practical support along the way — not to mention the inspiration she brought to the following pages. You know that the Holy Spirit speaks through spouses, right? Kathi has been telling me that for years — and in her case I think she's right.

I would also like to thank my parents, Douglas and Margaret Lowry, for their endless supply of wisdom and enthusiastic encouragement. Many of the ideas in this book have been shamelessly and gratefully acquired from them.

It has also been a pleasure working with Our Sunday Visitor. The mission of the organization, so necessary in today's world, provides hope and practical guidance to help us all become better Catholics. In particular, it has been a joy to work with Greg Erlandson, Bert Ghezzi, Kyle Hamilton, Linda Teeters, and Tom Blee, along with fellow authors Brandon Vogt, Kevin Vost, and Eric Sammons, as well as many others. Thank you so much for the opportunity.

The influence of the Columbus (Ohio) chapter of Legatus has also been enormous. I am so grateful to be part of the organization that it is hard to express this in words. Legatus is a huge asset to Catholic business leaders seeking greater integration of their faith and work. To Jo Ann and Chuck Wilson, Ellen and Alan Dekker, Lori and Tom Caldwell, Faith and Mike D'Andrea, Candy and John Gioffre, Peggy and Mike Hartshorn, Mary Ann and Stephen Jepsen, Ann and Jack Ruscilli, Joann and Dan Avramovich, Marian and Bob Schuda, David Karam, Warren Dazzio, Julie Naporano, and the rest of the board and members — thank you. You are all an inspiration.

Finally, many other friends have helped me along the way, including Marcus Grodi and the rest of the staff and board at The Coming Home Network, such as Father Ray Ryland, "Bog," et al. In addition, thanks to Mike Aquilina for being the first to encourage me to write, and for taking a chance on publishing several of my articles in *New Covenant* magazine. Mike, I owe you a beer. To Patrick Madrid, who published my conversion story in *Envoy Magazine* and *Surprised by Truth 2* — Pat, you're the man.

Scott and Kimberly Hahn were at the right place, at the right time, for Kathi and me during our conversion process — thank you. Also many thanks to Jon Wagner, Dick Kurth, Gary Irvine, Rob Rissmeyer, Stephanie McCloud, Joe Patrick, Ed Rivalsky, Tim Jakubisin, Don Materniak, James Harold, Regis Martin, Father Mike Scanlan, Jeff Rayis, Andy Molinari, Paul Thigpen, and everyone else with whom I have worked over the years who have all taught me so much.

> The LORD bless you and keep you!
> The LORD let his face shine upon you, and be gracious
>   to you!
> The LORD look upon you kindly and give you peace!
>   (Numbers 6:24-26)

Chapter 1

The High Calling of Work

How to Find Meaning in Our Work Through the Universal Call to Holiness

> *"Through work man must earn his daily bread and contribute to the continual advance of science and technology and, above all, to elevating unceasingly the cultural and moral level of the society within which he lives in community with those who belong to the same family."*
>
> Blessed John Paul II, *Laborem Exercens*
> ("On Human Work"), Introduction

What's Your Major?

Business . . . or the ministry? You have got to be kidding me! Who created these crazy tests, anyway?

I had just learned the results from my college aptitude tests. After answering one mind-numbing question after another for hours, the inexplicable results were in. The tests concluded, decisively, that my interests and background were perfect for a career in business . . . or the ministry. Say what?

This had to be my dad's fault. He was a Presbyterian minister, and a clerk of the General Assembly of The Presbyterian Church in Canada. However, he also received his Ph.D. in business from the Massachusetts Institute of Technology. What kind of combination is that? From my earliest years, I remember dinner-table conversations revolving around matters

15

of faith and business, and how to be a Christian in the work-place and the boardroom.

For me, the concept of going into ministry just didn't com-pute. My parents had been missionaries in Nigeria before I was born. Many years of my youth had been spent growing up in a manse, the house provided to the minister and his family by the local Presbyterian church. I had seen the ministry up close, and it definitely wasn't for me. Not very lucrative, and lots of people telling you what to do. It just wasn't appealing at all.

Now business, on the other hand . . .

Due to starting school early and later skipping a grade, my college career began at the age of sixteen. I attended Francis-can University of Steubenville, a small Catholic college in a different country, hours from home. Unfortunately, I was ill prepared for the rigors of college life, particularly the expecta-tion that I should actually attend classes. After overindulging in the social aspects of college, my academic career came to an abrupt halt in a mere three semesters.

Remedial Education

Dejectedly, I returned to my hometown of Toronto. Fortu-nately, within a short time, I found full-time employment with Sony of Canada, Ltd. For the first time, I was immersed in the world of business, first in information systems, later in market-ing. They could have paid me in product — high-quality TVs, home stereos, car stereos, etc.

I liked business! The work was challenging and dynamic, and my coworkers taught me a great deal about what I wanted to be — and didn't want to be — later in my career. Yet for my career to progress, I knew a degree was necessary. After three and a half years, it was time to return to school.

As it turned out, the only place on the planet that would consider me was Franciscan University. I re-enrolled, this time as a twenty-one-year-old with a strong work ethic and solid experience.

Even as a nominal Presbyterian, I had to take a certain number of Catholic theology courses in order to graduate. In many ways, this was like studying a foreign language. The culture, customs, and vocabulary were all strange to me. I didn't get how the pope was infallible. Or why Mary was so important. Or praying to dead people. None of it made sense.

However, through this process, I began to recognize the depth and beauty of many Catholic teachings. In particular, I took a course in ethics that studied the issue of artificial contraception — a complete nonissue for a Presbyterian. This was the tipping point in my appreciation of Catholicism.

Fast-forward

I am happy to say that the seeds planted in my heart and mind at Franciscan University have flourished since then in the so-called real world. Decades later, the "way of thinking" I discovered there has taken root and produced much growth. Not only did I end up converting to Catholicism — along with my beautiful wife, Kathi — but over the years I also became a CPA, picked up an MBA, fathered eight wonderful children, and became a business executive, board member, and speaker on topics of faith, work, and finances.

I've worked in several different organizations at various levels — everything from selling insulation door-to-door as a teenager, to being an accountant at a large CPA firm, to being a senior vice president at a large international company, to being executive vice president and chief operating officer at The Coming Home Network International, a small Catholic apostolate. In each position, I have worked hard, learned a great deal, and benefited from the experience. I have enjoyed working — not every day, for sure, but most.

In my case, business was the catalyst, but it has become apparent that part of my life's calling is to seek a greater understanding of how Christians can better integrate faith and work. Much to my surprise, the Catholic Church has the answers.

Now, you're familiar with the concept of getting a brilliant idea one day, right? It's like a lightbulb goes on above your head? Everything becomes clear in a momentary flash of brilliance, like the story of the Transfiguration?

This wasn't anything like that.

It took me well over twenty years of trial and error (mostly error), enduring many hardships, making countless mistakes, listening, reading, praying, thinking, and stressing out over work to come to a simple conclusion: **Our work provides one of the greatest opportunities we have to grow closer to God**.

All of Us Are on a Mission From God

Did you ever see the movie *The Blues Brothers*, where John Belushi and Dan Aykroyd talk about being on a mission from God? The fact is, we all are. Our work — whether it is in the business world, government, health care, homemaking, construction, day care, wherever — is central to our calling as Christians. On a practical level, work pays the bills, gives us an opportunity to interact with and use our talents for the benefit of others, and enables us to accomplish countless meaningful goals. On a societal level, work produces value in the form of goods and services, shared wealth (think highway infrastructure or national parks), and the means for individuals to better themselves.

The real opportunity, however, transcends even these lofty pursuits. The real opportunity is to sanctify our daily work, mostly the small stuff. After all, we can all go to work day after day, collect a paycheck every couple weeks or so, and gain at least some level of personal satisfaction. But isn't there really more than that? What if we could, regardless of the type of work we do, use the experience to fulfill God's plan, His purpose for our lives, and even draw others toward His kingdom? Is that possible?

My experience suggests that it is. Jesus tells us "If you love me, you will keep my commandments" (John 14:15). St. Paul tells us to "Rejoice always. Pray without ceasing" (1 Thessalonians 5:16-17). I don't know about you, but I usually spend well in excess of forty hours every week working. Scripture doesn't have any disclaimers with regard to the workweek — I haven't seen anything that says loving your neighbor as yourself only applies outside your regular workday.

One of the greatest challenges — and opportunities — in life is to allow our faith to permeate *every* aspect of our lives. Given a typical time allocation each week, not including weekends, most of us spend as much time at work as any other single pursuit. If we don't embrace our faith in the workplace, we're missing out on a huge opportunity.

Postmortem Retirement Planning

As a CPA, I have had quite a bit of experience with retirement planning. People routinely make sacrifices now in order to provide a comfortable retirement down the road. What if we take that same concept and apply it to a much longer-term goal — eternity! Don't we all aspire to a "comfortable" eternal retirement? It sure beats the alternative.

If we don't make our efforts at work into a form of prayer, and sanctify our daily work with perseverance each day, we are engaging in spiritual battle with one hand tied behind our back. It may be possible, but why even try? Why not give it everything we have, with the assurance that the Lord will guide our steps?

We don't just work for ourselves, or for an employer, or even for the good of all our stakeholders in life — we work for God.

As far as employers go, it doesn't get any better than that. The pay is rich, the benefits are phenomenal, and the retirement plan, to borrow a phrase, is out of this world.

ACTION STEPS

To sanctify your work, here are a few action items to consider building into your daily routine:

1. **Pray.** Daily prayer is essential and can include a dedicated prayer time, Scripture or religious reading, the Rosary (a personal favorite of mine), mental prayer during the day, and prayer specifically about our work. For example, I often bring work challenges to prayer, even as I seek to balance multiple priorities. To paraphrase Blessed Teresa of Calcutta, remember to pray for the grace to be not just successful, but faithful.

2. **Make a morning offering.** This is crucial — each day, we must make a new beginning in order to persevere until the end. Offer your day's work to God, and ask that He prosper your work — not just for you but also for the benefit of others. In addition, offer up your challenges and struggles, and ask for His blessing. Even when the circumstances seem dire, God is able to bring light out of any situation.

3. **Focus on the little things.** At times, heroic virtue might consist of biting your tongue rather than delivering a scathing response. It might mean putting aside your urgent priorities for a few minutes to help a coworker. It might mean just smiling at people and greeting them with a cheerful "Good morning!" — even when it feels like anything but.

4. **Do your best.** If we're really working for God, we should do our best to please Him, and to use our talents for His glory. Work well done is pleasing to God, even if we make

mistakes in the process. Remember, He can use all circumstances for good.

? QUESTIONS FOR REFLECTION

1. Do you see your work as part of God's calling for your life? Why or why not?

2. Do you know anyone who truly lives his or her faith effectively in the workplace? What do they do that is different?

3. What is one thing you could do immediately to be more faithful at work?

4. Is there anything (or anyone) driving you nuts in your workplace? How might a faith perspective change your behavior toward them?

5. What examples of a "little thing" done well have you seen in your past? How did it impact you or others?

Chapter 2

Maximizing Value

How to Go Beyond Shareholder Value and Consider Broader Stakeholders

> *"If we let Christ reign in our soul, we will not become authoritarian. Rather we will serve everyone. How I like that word: service! To serve my king and, through him, all those who have been redeemed by his blood. I really wish we Christians knew how to serve, for only by serving can we know and love Christ and make him known and loved."*
>
> St. Josemaría Escrivá, *Christ Is Passing By*

Shareholder Value

For many years, my greatest professional aspiration was to become a shareholder in my CPA firm.

I had seen others reach this goal after many years of tremendous sacrifice. It was always a time of great excitement around the office. Every year, there seemed to be more qualified candidates than openings, but for those who made it came financial rewards, great perks, and (perhaps just as important — to me, at least) a new car.

There was one shareholder in the firm, Chad, who had all the toys — beautiful vacation home, cars, bikes, boats, you name it. It came as a complete surprise when he mentioned to me one day, almost casually, that he was up to his eyeballs in debt.

So despite what I learned in business school about the importance of "maximizing shareholder value," I always

23

struggled with the concept in practice. No matter how hard I tried, and even though I knew Chad and liked him, it was impossible for me to get excited about making money for him.

Seeing Green

After getting married, and with a growing family, there always seemed to be financial needs. I took my role as provider very seriously, but we always seemed to have more children than money. We had three children (all under three years old) in a two-bedroom apartment for some time before we were able to afford — just barely — our first small house. We had serious medical issues with our third pregnancy, and again with our seventh child. It seemed that no matter how much money I made, we always needed more.

We relocated our family at the request of my firm, largely for financial reasons. There was a salary "sweetener" provided, along with speculation that the move might serve to accelerate my ascension to shareholder in the firm. We used to live forty-five minutes from our extended family, and the move meant we were almost three hours away. But we needed the money.

Money is important.

In fact, because I'm the sole provider for our family, money continues to be a visceral issue for me. Part of my role, and part of my self-worth, is derived from putting bread on the table for my family. And it's more than just bread! We have eight children, five boys and three girls. For a while, we had *four* teenagers at home. Our food budget was more than many people's mortgage payments.

Spiritual Values

But is money the most important thing? There is a saying: "Money is like air — you need a certain amount to live, but it isn't the reason for living."

As another old saying goes, "You can't take it with you." Scripture speaks of money in many instances, illustrating the need to put our trust in God above money: "Happy the rich person found without fault, / who does not turn aside after wealth" (Ben Sira [Sirach] 31:8).

Now, money isn't intrinsically evil, nor is its accumulation: "For the *love* of money is the root of all evils, and some people in their desire for it have strayed from the faith and have pierced themselves with many pains" (1 Timothy 6:10; emphasis added). It's putting money above God that gets us in trouble.

So if money isn't the ultimate value, what is? If, as Christians, we're trying to put our priorities in order and put God first in our lives, how do we do it?

We need to love and serve the Lord, and one another.

Can I Get Some Service, Please?

In a very concrete and practical sense, the highest value for Christians is service, which is the way we express our love. Happily, we are assisted in this task by the Holy Spirit, and therefore our poor efforts are given a huge boost. Service is really personified by Christ Himself, who gave everything for us. In a sense, we are all called to the same thing — serving our brothers and sisters in an effort to help them get to heaven. In the words of St. Paul, we "pour out" our very lives. Including at work.

As we go through our workdays, there are always opportunities for us to serve others. As we apply our faith to our work, even (perhaps especially) small things can be used by God for His glory. Little acts of kindness, a friendly smile, encouragement in times of difficulty — these can all be used by God to point the way to Him. We are the catalysts, and the Holy Spirit does the interior work in human hearts.

As Catholics, one of our most dearly held beliefs is that of the intrinsic value of the human person. We believe that *all* people are created by God and that Jesus died for the entire human family. Period. So when we enter the workplace, we need to apply this thinking. Each individual with whom we come into contact is, in a spiritual sense, an opportunity. Our job is to point all of them to Christ. By serving them.

"Non Serviam"

When Kathi and I moved to Columbus, Ohio, years ago, the economy was booming. Our house was something of a money pit and always seemed to need repair of some sort. We quickly learned that just getting someone to show up at the house was a minor miracle. After a while, we came up with a sarcastic phrase for these unresponsive repairmen: "How may I *not* help you?"

This contrasted sharply with my upbringing, where my parents had been servants in very real and practical ways for years. They were both generous spirits with a "service mentality." They genuinely cared about others, and they taught me to do the same.

In my career, I was privileged to work with extremely service-oriented firms. Of course, there was a profit motive, but this did not taint the fact that we were always striving to do our best for clients.

One of the legends of my firm had to do with the managing shareholder, Sam. A gruff, yet gold-hearted man, he had built up a substantial firm from nothing over a long and storied career. One day, one of the administrative assistants lost her purse, and Sam found her crying in the lunchroom. Despite deadlines and other pressing needs, Sam dropped everything and assisted the desperate woman in finding the purse. It took hours, but finally the wayward purse was found.

That story circulated throughout the firm and became part of the legacy handed down to successive classes of newly minted accountants. In fact, this firm legend taught me one of the most valuable lessons I have ever absorbed in the business world: *the importance of taking a sincere, personal interest in others.*

A Specialist Is Born

In my CPA firm career, specializing in various industries was important, since there were so many peculiarities associated with clients in certain industry groups. However, I soon found that true success required going one step further: specializing in each client. Taking a sincere, personal interest in a client (or prospective client) proved to be a winning strategy to building positive relationships and providing outstanding service.

If you think about it, service is possible regardless of our position. As a new staff accountant early in my career, my "calling" was to serve my supervisor and our client. Later, as a manager, it was to serve the shareholder and the client, along with the staff working with me on the engagement. As an executive, it was to serve my boss, our clients, and the people in my division.

You have probably heard the term "servant leadership" before. It's a leadership philosophy modeled on Jesus himself, who "did not come to be served but to serve" (Mark 10:45). The beauty of this approach is its universality — it can be used by anyone, anywhere. Its essence in practice is that all your stakeholders are there to be served. If you're a working mom, you have your husband, kids, boss, coworkers, customers, suppliers, etc. Each one, an opportunity to serve as Christ did.

A Shining Example

At this point, many of us say: "Well . . . how? I get pulled in multiple directions. It's impossible to serve everyone and make them happy. What am I missing?"

First, recognize the difference between serving and making people happy. Parents are called to serve their children in many ways, but I know from hard experience that my approach often results in something other than happiness. To love and to serve is all about doing what is best for the other from a practical and faith perspective. Striving for happiness just isn't enough — emotions are too fickle.

To improve our authentic service, I'm a fan of the incremental approach. Essentially, we should always be striving to serve better than we have before. Each day, we must pray for the grace to pull this off, since we need God's help. But growth in our faith demands increasing levels of self-sacrifice — the practical dying to self, the love that focuses not on one's own needs but on those of others. Not easy.

I know a woman who is a tremendous example of this approach. She is a physician, making a good living, yet lives a very simple life (much to the chagrin of her children). What does she do with her money? She donates it to various Catholic organizations.

What is her reward? A tax deduction, perhaps, and some satisfaction that she is using her money for worthy causes. But in the long run, how can the eternal value of her sacrifice be measured? Her love will have the effect of changing lives — a beautiful legacy indeed.

In the same way, we all have the ability to impact others, not necessarily through money, but through our words and actions. Have you ever met someone really important who was extremely gracious to you? I bet it left an impression, right? For example, I have met Cardinal John Foley and a few bishops, and they were extremely gracious people. Invariably, I found myself inspired. Our challenge is to be sources of grace for others!

So creating value really transcends making money. Not that money isn't important. It is. But building up the Kingdom is even more important, and for that we must *be* Christ for others. So be diligent, and take a personal interest in others and seek out opportunities to be sources of grace for them.

ACTION STEPS

To create eternal value, try these ideas:

1. **Pray for people**. Remember, every individual with whom we come into contact at work is an opportunity. Pray that God will lead their hearts toward Him, and that our humble efforts will be multiplied.

2. **Look for opportunities to serve**. The spectrum of human need is enormous, and we need to view these needs as opportunities to serve others. Although it seems paradoxical, the times people are often most open to Christ is when they are experiencing the greatest challenges in life. Especially during these times, look for ways to be a means of grace to them.

3. **Make small sacrifices**. One of the best ways to draw us closer to God is to make small sacrifices that only He knows about. This not only reminds us of our dependence on His grace, but it also helps us to appreciate the trials others face. Forgoing that second cookie at dessert and "offering it up" won't trouble anyone else, but it becomes a powerful tool in keeping our spirit receptive to God at all times.

4. **Be generous.** God loves a generous giver, and He can't be outdone in generosity. Consider using money as one way of investing in others rather than ourselves — this can be an antidote to the rampant materialism that surrounds us. After all, how can worldly trinkets compare to the treasures of heaven?

❓ QUESTIONS FOR REFLECTION

1. Do you look for opportunities during your workday to pray for others? Are there any people you work with who really need prayer?

2. What motivates you at work? Would you rather have a high-paying but terribly stressful job or be lower paid and content?

3. Are there any people you can think of who do a great job serving others? What do they do that is unique?

4. If your checkbook were audited, would it be obvious that you are Christian? Are your financial priorities in line with your faith?

5. How could you be more generous with people around you? Are there any opportunities you can think of that you could begin today?

Chapter 3

Get Me Off This Roller Coaster!

How to Integrate Work With Faith and Family Through a Plan of Life

> "To discover the plan of life that could render you fully happy, listen to God, who has a plan of love for each one of you. With trust, ask him: 'Lord, what is your plan, as Creator and Father, for my life? What is your will? I want to fulfill it.' Be sure that he will respond. Do not be afraid of his answer! 'God is greater than our heart and knows everything!' (1 John 3:20)."

> Pope Benedict XVI,
> 2010 World Youth Day Message

Is Balance Possible?

Balancing work and family obligations has always been a challenge for me. My desire to be a high achiever and my drive to provide for Kathi and our children have often resulted in me taking on ambitious (and time-consuming) projects.

Toward the end of my public accounting career, I was spending too much time at work. I remember driving home at nine o'clock at night, exhausted and feeling like an utter failure. It seemed like no matter how hard I tried, I wasn't spending enough time at work to succeed. At the same time, I wasn't spending enough time at home to succeed there either. Something had to give.

I had spent many years trying to manage the anxiety, stress, and long hours associated with life in a CPA firm. My "busy season" had expanded due to my involvement in nonprofit organizations, and the ever-growing client list provided a constant stream of challenges. Great for professional growth — not so good for a sustainable family life.

As it turned out, the Lord had a plan.

David

The struggle between work and family wasn't that unusual among my friends and coworkers, so I accepted it as being normal. But I had a wake-up call when Kathi was expecting our seventh child. At around twenty weeks, she knew something was wrong. After extensive testing, we found that our baby had a rare condition called Polysplenia syndrome — a congenital disease marked by the presence of several small, nonfunctioning spleens. We learned that the survival rate past adolescence was only 10 percent.

For the next several months, we were in mourning for our child who hadn't even been born yet. There was no assurance he would survive his birth. If he did, he would require surgery immediately, and there would be other issues surrounding the condition that would need to be managed.

So we prayed, along with many friends and family members. Well, the prayers were heard and answered — our son David was born *without* congenital heart disease, the primary cause of premature death among children with his condition. Praise be to God!

David did spend the first month of his life in the Neonatal Intensive Care Unit at Children's Hospital in Columbus. He weathered a surgery the morning after his birth, demonstrating an irrepressible spirit that continues to this day. We were incredibly grateful for the outcome, although the process had shaken us to the core.

Back to Basics

Although my CPA firm had been extremely supportive throughout Kathi's pregnancy, I still had to make a living. It didn't take long for me to begin working overtime again, but this time it wasn't sustainable. And Kathi and I knew it.

We decided to spend a couple of days at one of the beautiful state parks in Ohio — and although we had little David with us, grandparents watched the other children. We prayed a lot, and we spent time talking about our priorities. Just as important, we prayed fervently to determine God's will for our family.

As committed Catholics, we recognized the importance of keeping Christ at the center of our lives. Knowing God, loving Him, and serving Him are at the top of our priority list. Mass, daily prayer time, spiritual reading, regular confession, spiritual direction, the Rosary — all these things take time. God had to come first, we were sure of that.

We also identified our marriage and family as a key priority. Our family size wasn't going to get any smaller, so we had to arrange life in a manner that allowed for time together. Kathi and I had long enjoyed weekly date nights, and we tried to spend time with each of the children individually as well as together. This couldn't change, and we realized that the time commitment here would only increase in the future. Our marriage sacrament was (and is) God's manifest will for our lives. No question.

What about my career? As the sole breadwinner, I needed to make a reasonable salary in order to provide for the family. At the same time, I had these other priorities that weren't going away anytime soon. What could be done?

In the end, we decided it was time for us to take a leap of faith and make a career change. Despite the wonderful learning and growth opportunities in my firm, we decided that the CPA firm lifestyle involved too many hours away from the family. I still needed to make a decent living, but it would have to happen somewhere else.

God's Timing

Have you ever noticed that when God is leading us to change, things can fall into place better than anything we could have imagined? This is precisely what happened — within twenty-four hours of letting my firm know my decision, I learned about an opportunity that turned into a fantastic career move. While there were still plenty of ways to grow professionally in the new role, the hours were not nearly as extensive.

In retrospect, my busy schedule had clouded my thinking, and I hadn't always made the right decisions. It seems to be part of the human experience that when we have too many priorities vying for our attention, we don't always do a good job putting the right ones first. So we need to ask ourselves, "What is the most important thing?"

The *Catechism of the Catholic Church* says:

> God put us in the world to know, to love, and to serve him, and so to come to paradise. Beatitude makes us "partakers of the divine nature" and of eternal life. With beatitude, man enters into the glory of Christ and into the joy of the Trinitarian life. (CCC 1721)

So in practical terms, our top priority is to know God, and to strive for holiness by lovingly uniting our wills with His. Assuming that He didn't set us up for failure, it follows that *we always have time to do God's will.* If we don't have time to do everything, there are items on our to-do list that shouldn't be there, or shouldn't be there right now. The point is, our lives should follow a sense of calling, and this demands that we prayerfully discern, somewhat precisely, what God wants us to do. In this case, God's timing and will became clear as we prayed and followed.

Juggling Act

"Doing God's will" is sometimes easier said than done. Some women seem to be particularly vulnerable to a sense of self-imposed guilt if they can't "have it all," with a fulfilling schedule combining a career, marriage, children, faith life, hobbies, and sometimes even volunteer opportunities. Even with a gift for multitasking, the typical wife and mother trying to juggle these multiple priorities can soon become overwhelmed.

A friend of mine, Sherry, was trying to do all these things and more. In her mid-thirties, Sherry had a career, husband, two girls, was active in her church, and volunteered for a non-profit organization helping autistic kids, since one of her girls was on the autism spectrum. She even managed a hobby (boating) to get away from it all every now and then.

Sherry was very busy.

Unfortunately, there came a time when Sherry suffered from medical problems, and everything in her "have it all" life started crumbling around her. With Sherry sick, her husband had to stay home more, and this caused a loss of income due to his compensation being entirely commission-based. Her girls struggled in school. Church went out the window, and she was forced to back away from her volunteering. Even the hobby had to go. With Mom as the heart of the family, it was as if the family had suffered a "heart attack."

The good news is that through this difficulty, Sherry and her husband decided to make some changes. Obviously, the marriage was important, and part of God's calling for them. Same with the kids — no sending them back. Church was important, and it stayed on the list. But Sherry scaled back the volunteering and her career.

Just Say No

So one of the most important things in Sherry's case was to look critically at what she was doing and say no to certain non-essential activities. Of course, not everyone has the ability to scale back on his or her career, but Sherry did. It was a gift to the family, and everyone was grateful.

Just as important, however, is deciding what should be on the to-do list.

One of the best ways to order our priorities is to come up with a daily plan. I'm not talking about a checklist approach, where things are ticked off one after another and there is no spontaneity. This is an exercise in figuring out what is important, and in making sure the things that lead us to this goal are included.

Let's assume that you're attempting to allow your faith to lead your career efforts (after all, why else would you be reading this book?). If the most important job at work is to love and serve the Lord and others, the work itself must take on the character of a prayer. And if work is part of an integrated faith life, our daily plans include work and nonwork activities.

Daily Priorities

In order for our faith to be a vibrant part of our daily existence, we need prayer. This is the central means we have for ongoing communication with our Lord. Our prayers need not be complicated but instead simple, ongoing conversations with God, sharing our hearts with Him. In addition, Scripture reading is a way of maintaining God's perspective throughout our lives and of gaining wisdom and understanding. The Rosary is another prayer I cherish, given its scriptural basis and tremendous beauty.

As the source and summit of our faith, the Mass is an important priority. Of course, frequent confession is another avenue of tremendous grace. Need I even mention other spiritual reading, involvement in parish activities, or a regular retreat?

When I first became Catholic, trying to shoehorn all these things into my day seemed impossible. Now, years later, I have a tremendous appreciation for the value of a deliberate approach to life, as well as to work.

Here's an example of a pretty good day, at least for me. First, I get up right away and go running (physical exercise is another very important thing!). Afterward, I have prayer time, along with some Scripture reading. Then I get ready for work.

During my commute, I pray the Rosary and offer up my day's work. In addition, I pray for any particularly difficult situations and ask for the grace to act with love and wisdom. When I get to work, I may pray over my workload and ask for God's help setting priorities and getting things done on time. At noon, I might duck out for Mass or catch lunch with a friend or coworker.

Throughout the day, I'll say an occasional prayer asking for God's help, especially when things are crazy. At the end of the day, I'll pray prayers of thanksgiving for the things that went well, and I'll ask for assistance with those that didn't. If I'm lucky, it will be Friday night, and I'll have a date with my wife. Then we'll spend time with our children, playing cards, saying a decade of the Rosary, and maybe watching a movie.

Maintaining Perspective

At the end of the day, an examination of conscience is helpful, along with prayers for God's help in doing better the next day.

Again, the benefit of having this type of prioritized approach for your day is not to provide undue structure. Rather, it's to make sure that your daily activities reflect your deepest priorities. Note that this integration of faith into your workday is a seamless transition, since there really isn't a "transition" to speak of in your interior life — only in the external place and circumstances.

The daily plan is suitable for good times, bad times, and every time in between. After all, if you're not going to strive for holiness on a daily basis, when will you?

ACTION STEPS

To get off the roller coaster of excessive commitments and put God in the driver's seat, here are a few things to consider:

1. **Put God first.** If you can trust God with your very life and eternal salvation, you can certainly trust Him with your career. Prioritize your life to serve God first, and make your work an act of service to Him along with a way of serving others.

2. **Maintain spiritual practices when you're busy.** History is full of examples of extremely busy people who pray constantly and build other pious practices into their daily routine. The ultimate example is Jesus Himself, who, during His public ministry, frequently withdrew to spend time in prayer. You're not busier than Jesus, are you?

3. **Read Scripture regularly to maintain perspective.** Isn't it amazing how the Scriptures are constantly new and applicable? Sometimes when we're most troubled by things at work, reading Scripture can help us regain perspective.

4. **Have a plan.** Build a routine around the things that draw us closer to God. We know that God is always with us and that He cares about even the most mundane aspects of our lives. Our work is important to Him, so by offering it to Him as a form of prayer, we most effectively accomplish His will.

? QUESTIONS FOR REFLECTION

1. Is there anyone at your workplace who exemplifies "putting God first?" Is this done in a loud or a quiet manner?

2. Do you think of God during your workday? What are some ways that you can transform your work into prayer?

3. When is the last time you read a Scripture verse that spoke to a situation you were experiencing? How did this help you?

4. Do you have a plan for your work now? If so, what is the ultimate goal or highest priority?

5. Is there one thing you can think of that would be good to either exclude or include in your daily life in order to answer God's call to holiness?

Chapter 4

Who's on Your Team?

How to Be a Team Player Through Humility

> *"Following Jesus in His poverty, [the laity] are neither depressed by the lack of temporal goods nor inflated by their abundance; imitating Christ in His humility, they have no obsession for empty honors (cf. Galatians 5:26) but seek to please God rather than men, ever ready to leave all things for Christ's sake (cf. Luke 14:26) and to suffer persecution for justice sake (cf. Matthew 5:10), as they remember the words of the Lord, 'If anyone wishes to come after me, let him deny himself and take up his cross and follow me' (Matthew 16:24). Promoting Christian friendship among themselves, they help one another in every need whatsoever."*
>
> Decree on the Apostolate of the Laity
> (*Apostolicam Actuositatem*), 4

"*$%&@!^ Outstanding!"

If our faith is important to us, it should change us. We must evaluate our perspectives on God, sex, money, other people, work, and so on, not through the lens of human ideology but instead through the eyes of faith.

But it doesn't always begin like that.

When I was a young senior accountant, I recall my first interaction with the top technical guru at the firm. Joe was in charge of "QC" (quality control), and he reviewed every financial statement the firm audited. By reputation, Joe was a gruff, no-nonsense individual who valued accuracy and honesty. *Brutal* honesty.

So it was with great trepidation that I sent my first financial statement to QC. Even though the manager and shareholder had already signed off, the financial statements (or I) still had to go through Joe's buzz saw before they went out the door.

That afternoon, I was startled to hear Joe's voice as he strode down the hall. He was cussing loudly and rather excitedly. I couldn't tell if he was happy or upset. He paused momentarily at my cubicle. "Did you write this SOP 94-6 memo?" Wide-eyed, I managed a stammering "Y-y-yes. . . ." He abruptly continued down the hall to the manager's office.

I strained to hear the conversation. Amidst the colorful prose emanating from the manager's office, I caught a couple snippets of conversation. "*$%&@!^ outstanding!" "%@&#$! can actually write!"

A couple minutes later, I was invited into my manager's office to meet with him and Joe. The latter was standing beside the desk and immediately began to pepper me with questions. When had I started with the firm? What was my background before arriving? Where did I go to school? And most important, what was up with that memo? Although I was plenty flustered, I responded as best I could. It became obvious that Joe was very pleased. Once again, I heard him exclaim "*$%&@!^ outstanding!"

The Crucible

It was the beginning of one of the most intense learning experiences of my career. From that point forward, Joe made sure my professional life was full of challenges. He got me assigned to the messiest, most difficult clients possible. If there were unusual projects to be had, he would volunteer me for them.

It was like getting special attention from a Marine Corps drill sergeant.

Yet over the course of time, as Joe and I worked together, we became great teammates. He was a mentor to me, and he was always quick to impart the benefits of his wisdom and experience. For my part, I happily did my best on each assignment and strove to serve the client and live up to Joe's lofty expectations.

One client in particular caused me a great deal of consternation. There were several complex issues to deal with, including inventory anomalies and extensive litigation. But the biggest issue was Anthony, the company's controller. I thought that he was the most pompous, arrogant, foul-mouthed, rude, sexist, sanctimonious jerk I had ever met. When I found some errors in his inventory calculations, Anthony went on a rampage, and from that moment forward he did his best to disparage me at every turn. We just didn't like each other.

During the audit, I would frequently complain to Joe about Anthony's contemptible behavior. Joe and Anthony got along fine, so Joe didn't see things from my perspective at all. In fact, Joe was careful to remind me frequently about Anthony's intelligence and abilities. Of course, it didn't help. I couldn't stand the guy. It was a classic clash of personalities.

How Am I Doing?

At the end of the audit, Joe gave me the customary performance evaluation. Normally, my evaluations were positive, reflecting a determined work ethic and a desire to succeed in the firm. This time, not so much.

Joe ripped me apart.

After all my hard work, grinding through issue after issue, working long hours, not to mention dealing with Anthony, I was indignant. But Joe didn't let up. "You need to be able to get along with all of your clients, even the difficult ones," he said. "Anthony is smart and knows the business, but you didn't treat him very well." Ouch.

The poor evaluation really ate at me. Once I had calmed down a bit (which took a few days), I began to recognize that Joe had some valid points. However, my emotions weren't ready to let go. Anthony treated me like a kid. He was rude and disrespectful. Yes, he knew the business well, but I didn't trust him. I knew that he had complained to Joe about me.

I am sorry to say that these emotions continued to live on within me for several months, gradually giving way to bitterness and resentment. I blamed this on Anthony. He hadn't done me any favors. Who was he to mess around with my career? He was single and well off, while I had a family and was struggling to make ends meet. It just didn't seem fair.

The Turning Point

One day I got a call from Joe, who told me that Anthony's employer was selling the company. I was to spend the next few weeks assisting Anthony with the due diligence process. My heart sank. I wasn't ready for this.

Over the past few months, I had halfheartedly attempted to pray for Anthony and the situation. Now, with the new project beginning the next morning, my prayers went into overdrive. I couldn't sleep that night, and my mind raced as I battled negative emotions. Every fiber of my being didn't like Anthony, and here I had to work with him again, much sooner than I had planned.

The next day, I showed up at Anthony's office and attempted to make the best of it. We immediately got to work on some troublesome inventory issues, since there was huge time pressure to close the deal.

Over the next couple of weeks, something amazing happened. We ran into significant problems with the inventory calculations. Working together, we were able to work through one problem after another. Finally, the process was complete.

I had been praying for Anthony the whole time, partly out of obedience — "But I say to you, love your enemies, and pray for those who persecute you" (Matthew 5:44) and partly out of sheer desperation. During the due diligence process, we had been forced to work together under difficult circumstances and high stress levels. By the end, most of the negative emotions had evaporated, and I found that there was indeed a basis for respect. Anthony might never become my best buddy, but he was a smart guy. His attitude had also come around, and we actually got along pretty well. It was a bit surreal.

End or Beginning?

In the end, Anthony and I actually became friends. A year or so after the sale of the company, Anthony needed some tax work done on a personal business — and he called me. What a turnaround! By God's grace, the relationship that was so poor at first, with so much mutual bad blood, no trust, and active animosity, was healed.

Joe was right.

It was a major milestone in my personal career development, and a new beginning in how I regarded others. Instead of a competitive attitude toward clients or coworkers, I learned to look for their talents. As it turned out, this was also an important element of management, since achieving success through others requires recognizing and cultivating their particular strengths. Anthony's talents, although different from mine, were very real and very strong.

I was reminded of this reality years later, when hiring a corporate controller for the company where I was vice president of finance. Laura came to the company with a much different background than mine. It became clear that while I was the "big picture" guy, she was very attentive to detail. In fact, we were different in so many ways, it became humorous. One day in preparation for an offsite training seminar, we took psychological tests that showed our profiles to be exact mirror opposites.

Laura was among the best hires I ever made. Where I was weak, she was strong, and vice versa. Although very close in age, even our personal lives were completely different. The funny thing was that it worked extremely well, since we respected each other's strengths.

Complementary Perspectives

The experience with Anthony was the catalyst to increase my appreciation for the value of complementary perspectives among team members. Joe had done me a huge favor in helping me to see Anthony as someone who was worthy of respect, first by example and then by calling me out on my poor attitude. Honest correction of others isn't easy, even for a gruff son of a gun like Joe, but it sure is important.

The fact is, we're all smart in different ways. Joe was smart technically, and he was also a really good judge of talent — of all types. Anthony, as it turned out, had an acute business sense and good judgment, despite his highly developed bravado. In a way, it reminded me of Scripture's exhortation to appreciate unity in the Body of Christ, while embracing a diversity of gifts: "I . . . urge you to live in a manner worthy of the call you have received, with all humility and gentleness, with patience, bearing with one another through love, striving to preserve the unity of the spirit through the bond of peace" (Ephesians 4:1-3).

In practice, the only way to really pull this off is suggested in the Scripture passage. It's a rare, radical, and almost foreign way of thinking. We don't see enough contemporary examples around us, since it tends to be quiet and unobtrusive. The way of thinking is the way of humility.

Now why is this so rare, and so radical? We see examples of pride all around us, shouting from the media, offering self-sufficiency as an ideal, turning us inward to focus on ourselves. Yet it is humility that Christ demands from us.

Mea Culpa

In my interactions with Anthony early on, you might have noticed that it was all about me. How I appeared to Joe. How I didn't like being treated with disrespect. How I didn't care for someone who had different values from me. Me, me, me.

Humility demands that we step out of ourselves and instead focus on others. Once I began to pray for Anthony, and once my emotions cooled to the point where the Holy Spirit was able to work in my heart, I discovered Anthony's positive qualities. In a sense, humility was the foundation for the healing of the relationship. It was no longer about me, but a happy side effect in the end was that I benefited as much as Anthony!

In working with management teams over the course of time, I have seen many examples of humility facilitating team-work. Humility is the virtue that enables us to appreciate the value of others, to overcome the inevitable bruises we sustain in our work lives, and to strive to serve in imitation of Christ.

Conversely, ego is quick to disable a team. Think of the successful company cultures you see in action. Chances are, at the core of the company are people committed to a common goal, lending diverse talents to make it work. Greed and narcissism can appear to succeed in the short term, but never in the long term — and certainly not in the eternal sense.

ACTION STEPS

To be a better team player, and to strive to serve others as Christ did, try the following:

1. **Look for talents in others.** Like Joe, we can be of great service to others by recognizing and encouraging their talents — even if it involves the occasional reprimand. Investing our own time, talents, and treasure in others can yield bountiful results.

2. **Use hurdles as stepping-stones.** The workplace is full of hurdles, or it wouldn't be work! By our willingness to accept challenges gracefully, we become ever more open to following God's calling in our lives. Challenges make us stronger!

3. **Read the Bible and other spiritual books.** One of the best ways to maintain daily perspective is to read. This is a great way to allow God to speak to us, as His words are ever new and can be applied to current situations.

4. **Be humble.** Humility is the foundation of spiritual development, and it holds untold spiritual and practical benefits. Even small steps yield big results, and there are ample opportunities to exercise this virtue in the workplace!

5. **Pray for your teammates.** If there's anyone in particular who irritates you, pray for him or her every day. This benefits the team, and it has the power to transform our own hearts.

? QUESTIONS FOR REFLECTION

1. Have you ever had someone recognize your talents? What happened, and how did this make you feel?

2. Describe a challenge you have overcome that led to good things in your career. How have you benefited from the situation?

3. Do you read Scripture or other spiritual writings on a regular basis? How does this help you in your daily work?

4. Have you seen any instances of humility in the workplace? Give an example.

5. Describe the qualities of good teams in your workplace. How does this impact the overall organization?

Chapter 5

An Attitude of Gratitude

How to Maintain a Spirit of Gratitude in All Circumstances

"Rejoice always. Pray without ceasing. In all circumstances give thanks, for this is the will of God for you in Christ Jesus."
1 Thessalonians 5:16-18

Today Is Your Last Day

I was in shock. As if I had just been punched unexpectedly, there was a pit deep in my stomach, adrenaline pumping through my veins, and sweat on my forehead. My mind raced — what had just happened? I had tried to do the right thing, giving plenty of advance notice before leaving my CPA firm in order to relocate to the Pittsburgh area. But there I was, jobless. The firm didn't need me for the transition period as I anticipated. Today was to be my last day, and I had been unceremoniously invited to pack up my things and leave by the end of business. Now we wouldn't have enough money to pay for necessities over the next few weeks. Necessities like food.

With all the courage I could muster, I called Kathi. She was at home with our four children, the oldest of whom was five years old at the time. As you might imagine, the conversation didn't go well. She cried. Money was really tight. We had budgeted carefully and done everything we could to plan the move that would bring us closer to our families who lived in the Steubenville, Ohio, area. I tried to console her, and quietly determined that I had to do something. I felt angry, betrayed, and humiliated. My naïveté had cost us, big time.

Don't Take It Personally

From my boss's standpoint, this was a simple business decision. I was a senior accountant and therefore relatively low on the totem pole. The firm could shift work around and save the cost of my salary. It wasn't a big deal. They would have to replace me anyway, so why not invest in the next person instead? It made perfect sense. "Don't take it personally," he said.

Unfortunately, while understandable in the cold light of economic reality, this put me in a real pickle. How would I provide for the family until I started my next job? As the sole provider, this really hit me at a deep level — much of my self-worth, probably too much, was wrapped up in my ability to provide for Kathi and our growing family. My salary at the time was modest, we had debts and bills to pay, and we didn't even have much access to credit in order to ride out the storm.

God, Are You Serious?

I drove home that day in a daze. Attempting to make sense of the situation, my prayers were fervent and, reflecting an immature and self-centered faith, somewhat indignant: "God, how could You do this to me? I was acting in good faith. I was making this move for the right reasons. I was trying to put others' needs ahead of my own."

Thankfully, this line of thinking quickly fizzled and gave rise to more reflective thought. God had led us through trials before, so why should I doubt now? We had many benefits others didn't have — supportive family, friends, and a secure job waiting in Pittsburgh. Some of my close friends didn't have jobs at all, or they were experiencing profound struggles with their marriage, illness, or the loss of family members. My troubles were paltry next to them. "The fundamentals are in good shape," I told myself. "God will provide."

Kathi and I talked late into the night. Although the sting was still fresh, Kathi had managed to absorb the news a bit better. With characteristic love and support, she encouraged me to persevere: "God will show us the right path. Hang in there. Let's pray about it." And pray we did.

The Turnaround

The next day, I woke up early and prayed earnestly: "God, please help us. You have always taken care of us. I trust You." For good measure, I prayed the Rosary, my favorite prayer. Then I began making phone calls. Former clients, friends, business associates, you name it. One call in particular went well — I had been the controller for a health care company before going back into the CPA-firm world, and Ed, the owner of the company, agreed to talk to me. I went over to meet with him that afternoon.

The substance of the meeting was a blur. I explained the situation and offered to do anything he needed on a consulting basis. Even though he had long since replaced me as his controller, I still recall his attitude of compassion and understanding. I'm pretty sure he manufactured a project for me on the spot, and I left with a check in hand for more than the shortfall. It was all I could do not to break down in tears. Within twenty-four hours, I had gone from the depths of despair to the pinnacle of thanksgiving.

It's Not Easy Being Me

It would be easy to assume that the above story is about me. At the time, I certainly thought it was. It's difficult to step outside yourself even in the best of times, much more so when you're going through some difficulty. But as it turned out, the story wasn't about me at all. Just like the parable of the Prodigal Son in the Gospel (Luke 15:11-32), it would be understandable for many of us at first glance to think the story is about the son who takes off and spends his father's fortune. It's really more about the father, and how the father's actions instruct us about God's love for us.

The story is really about Ed.

Another Perspective

Ed understood when I approached him that I was stressed out. He also understood that it wasn't the do-all-to-end-all crisis and that perhaps I was reacting emotionally more than rationally. So what did he do?

Ed recalled during our meeting the years I had spent as controller of his company. He described how I had always tried my best and that he appreciated my dedication and loyalty. He expressed his gratitude, and as if to prove it, he handed me a check.

Here's where it gets interesting. For Ed, this entire episode wasn't a big deal. He acted in a way that was consistent with his character. The check he paid me would get him value from a business standpoint, and he was happy to help out.

The Healing Power of Gratitude

The impact on me, on the other hand, was profound. This event occurred very early in my career, and I remember it like it was yesterday. I remember the amount of the check. I remember how I felt, the extraordinary sense of relief and thankfulness. Ed and I have worked together many times on projects since that time, and we have gone through thick and thin. He has my everlasting gratitude because of this act of generosity. *I will never forget it.*

Ed's gratitude for my faithful and effective work helped heal me.

Jesus understood that life deals out its share of pain. When He was physically present on earth, He allotted a fair bit of His time to healing others. In fact, He allowed Himself to be "inconvenienced" on many occasions, leaving situations where He was teaching to help someone in need. In a similar manner, although Ed probably had other pressing matters to deal with the day he met with me, he took time to be inconvenienced and to provide relief.

Since we are all called to imitate Christ, shouldn't we also desire the healing of others? Think of Jesus' words to the woman afflicted with a hemorrhage: "Daughter, your faith has saved you. Go in peace and be cured of your affliction" (Mark 5:34). By our gratitude toward others, in a less dramatic way, we are able to contribute to their healing and send them off in peace.

Gratitude and Loyalty

Ed's gratitude also engendered a profound loyalty within me. I will always be in his debt. His simple act touched me at a deep level at the right time, and I will always be thankful.

Now, isn't this an opportunity? Think of those around us who are going through difficulties at any given point in time. What if we regard those difficulties as opportunities to make a "deposit" of gratitude? What if we are vigilant in seeking out qualities in others for which we should be grateful?

For my part, gratitude was something I completely missed. In the whirlwind of events, gratitude wasn't on my list. Wasn't this a missed opportunity on my part? Shouldn't my attitude toward God reflect a complete and unrelenting thankfulness, even in the worst of times? There are no guarantees that circumstances in this life will get better, but just look at what Jesus says in Scripture about the eternal rewards to those who are faithful.

The ability to be consistently grateful to God, even during difficult times, is a rare quality, even among Christians. However, it's what our faith requests of us.

And we can take some steps to foster our gratitude. For example, several years ago, I remember my kids fighting among themselves. A lot. It was driving me crazy. As a result, Kathi and I came up with a new approach: each evening after dinner, we started to "go around the table" and each of us would say what we were thankful for on that particular day.

Over the course of time, almost imperceptibly, the kids became less negative toward one another. It wasn't like flipping a switch, of course, but gradually the kids began looking for positives and became less focused on the negatives. Next, we began praying a decade of the Rosary together every night. Our prayer time continues to move in the direction of gratitude toward God, and loyalty to one another.

Gratitude and Relationships

Another fascinating aspect of gratitude is its impact on relationships. For example, at one point I took on a new direct report at work. She was interested in my perceptions about her, and I explained that I was grateful that she now reported to me. "You have a tremendous skill set — you're smart, loyal, and extremely technically savvy. Beyond that, I admire your stability through the many changes that have gone on in the company." My comments were sincere, and the relationship flourished.

I have a couple of friends who became very wealthy in their forties and fifties. What is interesting about these situations is that in each case, the individuals emerged with a more pronounced appreciation of our need for others. "It's all about relationships," my one friend says.

I once heard that the best way to build relationships is through respect and affection, and the best way to destroy them is through contempt. Respect is expressed well through gratitude, particularly in the workplace. We can always find things that are worthy of gratitude if we're willing to seek them out.

ACTION STEPS

If we are to be grateful and make this a part of our daily practice, here are a few things to keep in mind:

1. **Be grateful even when you don't feel like it.** Gratitude should trump our feelings. Emotions can be a poor guide to behavior at times, and if we wait until we feel grateful, we may never express gratitude enough.

2. **Practice gratitude through good and bad times.** Scripture tells us to "Rejoice in the Lord always. I shall say it again: rejoice!" (Philippians 4:4). There is a beauty we can see in those who develop a genuine "attitude of gratitude" and learn to express it regardless of external circumstances. It is a discipline, a way of thinking, and a learned habit. But it's not like lifting weights or going on a diet — it's an opportunity to lift up others and heal them, providing them with the Lord's peace and offering them a reflection of His love.

3. **Focus on what you have, not what you don't have.** Gratitude, by its nature, is a response to what we have, not what we don't have. We have a tendency in our society to become overly focused at times on what we want. Think of gratitude as the antidote to disordered materialism and aversion to work. Recall my wealthy friends, who after settling all financial worries, looked around to figure out what else matters. Their conclusion: people.

4. **Focus on God first, then on others.** Gratitude is extraordinarily attractive. Notice that we are drawn almost intuitively toward those who habitually express gratitude.

Have you ever seen sports figures credit teammates for outstanding play? We appreciate their humility and think more highly of them. In an even deeper sense, think of what the Lord has offered us — the gift of Himself, the gift of eternal salvation. If we focus on Him, gratitude is a natural response.

? QUESTIONS FOR REFLECTION

1. Do you know people who have a real "attitude of gratitude"? What are they like?

2. What are some ways to express gratitude in your workplace? Have you tried this? If so, what were the results?

3. Have you ever experienced healing through the power of gratitude? How so?

4. Do you think loyalty is enhanced through gratitude? Has this happened to you?

5. How can you put the corporal works of mercy into action in your workplace?

Chapter 6

Give Me Patience, Quick!

How to Positively Impact Your Work by Trusting God . . . and Waiting

> *"Do not say, 'I will repay evil!'*
> *Wait for the LORD, who will help you."*
>
> Proverbs 20:22

The Waiting Is the Hardest Part

Stephanie is a good friend of mine who spent many years working in state government. An attorney by training, she is by nature a cheerful individual, strong in faith, and powerful in intellect. Stephanie and her husband Brad (also an attorney) have two children, a dog, and a mortgage. By most external standards, Stephanie is pretty normal.

Don't read this too loudly, but she's also (shhh . . .) both a Christian and a Republican.

A couple years ago, the Democratic Party was on the upswing, and during a general election many Republicans were kicked out of office. At that time, Stephanie was chief counsel to the state's Republican attorney general. Much to her chagrin, the Democratic challenger won the election. As soon as the results were in, she began to hold her breath.

Brad also worked in state government for a Republican who lost the election. Unfortunately, he didn't have time to hold his breath. Because Brad had announced he would be campaigning as a Republican in a suburban mayoral race, he was unceremoniously fired almost immediately. What used to be a two-income household was now one.

Stephanie describes the weeks following the election as some of the most stressful in her life. Despite being attorneys, she and Brad did not have deep financial resources to fall back upon, having dedicated most of their careers to public service. In addition, with Brad out of a job, the pressure was squarely on Stephanie to provide. If Stephanie lost her job too, they could lose their house.

So they waited.

Prayer Really Works

Throughout this uncertain time, Stephanie recalls praying fervently — and frequently. "It was one of the most trying times of my life. I even had sores inside my mouth caused by the stress." The physical manifestations of the inward reality served to emphasize how personal a struggle this was for Stephanie. Even with her awareness of God's faithfulness, she experienced a deep and prolonged anxiety.

The weeks passed, and Stephanie continued to strive to do her best at work, all the while expecting the other shoe to drop. While others in her office were resigned to the changes, or bitter about the impact on themselves and their families, Stephanie determined to make the best of the situation. She committed herself to doing her best as always, despite the circumstances. She also resisted the urge to "hide her light" and pretend to be something she wasn't. Finally, the new attorney general took office and evaluated his staff. As expected, many good attorneys and other staff were let go.

But not Stephanie.

For his part, Brad still wasn't able to find many good career alternatives as a Republican government attorney in a state now run by Democrats. He wound up taking some freelance work to make ends meet. Despite Stephanie maintaining her employment, the future was still uncertain, and the entire family felt the pressure. They continued to pray, although their emotions were running high and some days it didn't feel that they would ever get through this difficult time.

Yet their prayers were heard. During that year, Brad ran the race for mayor — and won a difficult and contentious election. Stephanie also found a new career in the private sector as general counsel for a workers' compensation company. She heard about the position through a friend — a Democrat!

Instant Gratification — Not!

So what's the moral of the story? Republicans should only marry Democrats and vice versa?

Of course not. What Stephanie did right in this process was to trust, pray, and persevere in faith while continuing to do her best. She was patient, and she waited for the Lord.

Now, it's easy to talk about this whole episode in retrospect, after things had settled and the uncertainty had been resolved. But recognize that *the entire process took over a year to unfold.* That's a lot of sleepless nights, staring at the ceiling, and imploring God for help. These situations take time! Fortunately, we know that God can bring good out of even the most excruciating circumstances: "We know that all things work for good for those who love God, who are called according to his purpose" (Romans 8:28).

The difficulty is in anticipating God's grace while we're in the midst of the excruciating circumstances. As we know from hard experience, these difficulties sometimes last even longer than a year. And God is not known for accepting all of our suggestions as to timing and desired outcomes. He loves us too much for that.

Scripture speaks of a different way God deals with us. Out of sheer love (because God *is* love), He allows us to live in the crucible of hardship. This is referred to often, particularly in the Old Testament, using the imagery of a refining fire: "See, I refined you, but not like silver; / I tested you in the furnace of affliction" (Isaiah 48:10). Uncomfortable? You bet! Spiritually profitable? Beyond our wildest dreams.

All Politics Is Local

Stephanie later found out that the new attorney general, despite being of a different political persuasion, valued her professionalism and reputation for integrity. To him, these factors transcended her Christian and conservative views (which he did not share in any way). When she left the office, the two parted as friends and remain so to this day.

For Brad's part, if it weren't for losing his job, he wouldn't have been able to dedicate the time needed to run for mayor — a definite step up for his career. In the long run, if he ever wanted to return to state government, his credibility would now be far higher with the mayoral experience.

So in both cases, things turned out for the best. But there's more to the story.

Why did Stephanie keep her job?

We could conclude that God answered her prayers. But would this have been the case if Stephanie had a poor attitude toward her new boss, or her dedication under a new regime suffered? Part of our role in cooperating with God's grace is to do our best, even in the context of trials and tribulation. Stephanie cooperated with grace by remaining true to her "core values" and entrusting her life (including her career) to God throughout the process. Despite the uncertainty and accompanying emotions, Stephanie remained gracious, professional, and effective in her role. The new attorney general may have heard "Christian and Republican," but what he saw was integrity and competence.

Faithfulness, Not Success

Let's face it. Our ultimate goal is to hear the words "Well done, my good and faithful servant" (Matthew 25:23). Our goal is to serve God first, and to love our neighbor as ourselves. The desired effect is to spend eternity with God, and to bring as many people along as possible! In order to pull this off, we need to place our trust in the Lord ahead of our fickle emotions. Patience and joy during difficulties speak volumes to coworkers.

As Catholics, we are given the tools to live a sacramental life — and the sacraments provide the grace for us to love others. Period, full stop. Regardless of belief, color, creed, socioeconomic status, whatever. Even if they're Republicans and we're Democrats, or vice versa!

Recall the example of Blessed Mother Teresa of Calcutta, who inspired millions around the world as she poured out her life for the poorest of the poor. Incredibly, as we know, she also accomplished these great works in spite of long periods of profound spiritual dryness. She didn't care whether the people she helped were Hindu, Muslim, or Christian. She loved them all, and she reminded us that our goal is faithfulness, not success. The same is true at work. We may be the only exposure to Christ our coworkers ever have.

When we enter the workplace, we aren't always in a position to quote Bible verses or to illustrate our points with citations from encyclicals. But we're always able to conduct ourselves with virtue and honor. In fact, many of the popular business books on the market today essentially repackage eternal truths, and these truths help us to harmonize our faith and work. There are many examples of those who are quick to criticize errors by management or others, but we tend to be less adept at identifying opportunities — especially for ourselves — to love and affirm others. Such opportunities abound.

Think also of how we hear various organizations passionately describing how they value their employees, customers, or whomever. We should be able to support this stance wholeheartedly! It sounds like Catholic teaching — and although these truths are articulated using secular language, they fit neatly with our belief of ascribing a high value to the dignity and intrinsic worth of the individual.

ACTION STEPS

We need plenty of grace to maintain a spirit of trust in the midst of workplace challenges. Here are a few ideas to help us all be part of the solution, not the problem:

1. **Pray, persevere, and do your best.** In today's environment, the rate of change and resulting uncertainty is at an all-time high. When you are confronted with these realities, view them as an opportunity to grow in faith and hope. Offer your daily work to God and do your best, recognizing that He can take any set of circumstances and use them for His glory — even when it takes a long time.

2. **Put faithfulness ahead of success**. God must come first, before our organizations. Nothing we do at work should contradict our faith, or put us in a position where we value money, status, or whatever above people. Part of being faithful is loving others as ourselves, and we have the ability to do this in practical ways every day.

3. **Love others, no matter who they are**. One of the hallmarks of those who have ascended to positions of great influence is that of graciousness toward others. Even when there are deep and significant ideological or religious differences,

the universal call to holiness demands a loving approach. While we are experts at identifying shortcomings in others, we could all do a bit better recognizing and affirming their virtues and trusting the Holy Spirit to change their hearts.

4. **Put faith first**. Regardless of political affiliation or worldview, our faith should be the driving force of our lives. To paraphrase an old slogan, think of it this way: My work life, *powered by Jesus Christ*. Individual human hearts are the target audience; we just sow the seeds and let God do the rest.

❓ QUESTIONS FOR REFLECTION

1. Do you know any coworkers who demonstrate a consistent professionalism regardless of the circumstances? Describe an example.

2. Are there any coworkers you know who have gone through tremendous difficulties in their work or personal lives, and everything has turned out for the best? What happened?

3. Have you ever met someone at work who exuded a love for others and graciousness that is instinctively attractive? How did this impact you?

4. Do you see divergent political viewpoints as causing division among people at work? Is there any way to overcome this in practical terms?

5. Describe one person at work you could affirm immediately. How will you do it?

Chapter 7

How to Treat the Janitor

How to Treat Others With Dignity and Respect at Work

> *"We come to a full sense of the dignity of the lay faithful if we consider* the prime and fundamental vocation *that the Father assigns to each of them in Jesus Christ through the Holy Spirit: the vocation to holiness, that is, the perfection of charity. Holiness is the greatest testimony of the dignity conferred on a disciple of Christ."*
>
> Blessed John Paul II, *Christifideles Laici* ("Christ's Faithful People"), 16 (emphasis in original)

James

I recall my dad telling me very early in my career that you can tell a lot about an organization by how the president treats the janitor.

So there I was (during my hiatus from college) at Sony of Canada Ltd., trying to learn the ropes and getting to know people. My position as computer operator was not glamorous. I personified the bottom rung of the ladder. Everyone else in the company outranked me, except a man named James.

James was the janitor. I saw him whenever I worked the evening shift, as we were among a small number of employees working during those hours. James was an older gentleman (from an eighteen-year-old's perspective), perhaps in his fifties, with a thick Jamaican accent. I noticed immediately that he

was *very* slow. In his movements, his speech . . . he did everything *slowly*.

James probably wouldn't have scored very well on intelligence tests. He wasn't very articulate or charismatic, nor was
he in good physical shape. In fact, there was only one thing he
did that I remember clearly: when I saw him, he would always
smile and say, "Hello! How are you?" That was usually it.

The President

One day, I happened to be walking down the hall and saw the
president of the company, Daniel, approaching James. Much to
my amazement, Daniel stopped and addressed James by name,
shook his hand, and patted him on the back. I overheard a bit
of the conversation, just small talk, with Daniel asking how
James was feeling and thanking him for always doing a good
job. The whole conversation probably only took a few seconds.

I was blown away.

Two aspects of this simple encounter have stuck with me
ever since I witnessed this brief, seemingly unremarkable
interaction.

First, it was an utterly striking juxtaposition, seeing these
two individuals with completely different roles, and realizing
that both were using their gifts while serving the organization.

Second, I was impressed with Daniel treating James with
honor and respect, and taking a personal interest in him — and
vice versa! This is what we Catholics refer to as the "dignity of
the person." Daniel and James transformed this principle into
action right before my eyes.

Dignity and Respect

There are few things as powerful in creating a positive environment as treating others with dignity and respect. This is a

way in which we recognize Christ within each individual, even when the image may appear grossly distorted by sin. Recall Jesus taking heat (as usual) from the Pharisees in Mark's Gospel. They asked, "Why does he eat with tax collectors and sinners?" Jesus' reply is relevant to this day: "Those who are well do not need a physician, but the sick do. I did not come to call the righteous but sinners" (Mark 2:17). Note that throughout the Gospels, Jesus treats *all* people with love and respect, inviting them to follow Him. Shouldn't we do the same?

Now, I have no idea whether James and Daniel were Catholic. Yet each was modeling the kind of behavior we should all aspire to. This is one practical manifestation of the second great commandment, to love our neighbor as ourselves. It goes beyond avoiding hurt to others. It even goes beyond treating others politely. To truly fulfill our duty to love, we are called to treat them with *honor*.

Compound Interest

Another powerful tool is our ability to take a sincere, personal interest in others. Not only does this fulfill the goal of loving and honoring others in a habitual manner, but it also makes it personal.

At Sony, Daniel had taken a personal interest in James. Due to Daniel's stature in the company, this kind of behavior was emulated by others and characterized the culture of the organization. This culture of treating people well was one of the reasons for the company's success.

I can attest to the fact that James was a terrific janitor. He did a great job, which in his case meant paying attention to detail and taking "ownership" of his areas of responsibility. Furthermore, he added intangible value to the company by being so congenial toward others. I still have positive memories of James, years later, for his smiles and greetings. He was using his God-given gifts and applying them to his job in a simple, yet profound way.

Senior Leadership

One of the greatest examples of leadership in my life was my grandmother.

Grandma lived to ninety-six years of age, and she was one of the strongest women I've ever met. She had a remarkable intellect and power of will, the latter borne from many years of hardship including rearing six children alone. She was the first woman ever in her family to attend college and was among the founders of the Canadian Guild of Industrial, Commercial and Institutional Accountants.

I was quite pleased to be the subject of Grandma's interest as a child. Through her example, and our countless discussions, I recognized the importance of lifelong learning.

Grandma was determined to learn something new every day. She loved talking to people, even those with whom she disagreed, and drawing out their opinions. She valued writing as a way of helping others. Over the years, I adopted many of her ideas as my own, only later to recognize that they could be traced back to her work as an accountant!

Hey, Joe

This type of leadership leaves a mark. I saw it again later in my professional career, when my mentor Joe went out of his way to teach me difficult concepts or share his perspective on business situations. Of course, there was a business benefit involved, but the intangible value of Joe's patient and encouraging approach was enormous. As you can imagine, he earned my admiration and loyalty in the process.

In retrospect, the greatest gift I received from Joe was the gift of his time. This was the way he demonstrated, in tangible terms, his commitment to my professional development. It was a sincere, personal compliment that resulted in me feeling honored and appreciated, since I knew Joe had many other pressing priorities.

The other thing I learned from watching Joe was that taking an interest in individuals can extend to any relationship. This approach can be used with bosses, colleagues, employees, clients, sales prospects, vendors, and even competitors.

But here's the caveat. In order for this approach to be effective, our motivation must go beyond simply accomplishing business objectives. If we're not sincere, if we're "using" people in a utilitarian manner, our "interest" in others will ring hollow. However, with the motivation of faith, desiring to love others as Jesus loves us, we can accomplish spiritual objectives and business objectives simultaneously.

I have a friend, Sarah, who excels at taking a sincere and faith-filled interest in others. Like me, she has a questionable memory. As a result, she crafted a system whereby she kept meticulous written records on people she met in a professional capacity: all the regular contact data, of course, but also information on family, hobbies, birthdays, professional interests, associations, and so on.

Originally, this was a business-motivated system. Over time, however, Sarah began to see how valuable it was to encourage others along the path of business and life itself. She would send relevant articles to people from magazines or the Internet, cards with a personal note on birthdays — and this was great for business. Then she decided to begin praying for them as well. Not only did this lead to good business opportunities as originally intended, but it also resulted in strong relationships that transcended business.

Relationship Bridge

There is a constant need in our workplaces to build bridges with others who are different from us. We may work with people of the opposite sex, different religious or ethnic backgrounds, and even those who are openly hostile to us. How do we treat people in these situations?

While all of us are individuals, and should be treated as such, we are also worthy of being treated with love and honor. There may be instances where someone's treatment of us makes it more challenging to uphold the principles of our faith, but these provide an opportunity for us to grow. Our focus always needs to remain on acting with a spirit of true Christian charity — focused on the other, and praying for God's grace in the difficult situations. So regardless of who they are or what the circumstances, we should treat others with love and honor, recognizing their intrinsic worth as children of God.

ACTION STEPS

To build strong relationships and mirror Christ at work, try the following:

1. **Pray for others.** For both good and bad relationships, pray for the grace to treat others with a spirit of true charity. Strive to recognize Jesus in others, and act accordingly. Quick aspirations (short prayers) on the fly during your workday work beautifully!

2. **Treat everyone with honor.** Go beyond courtesy: let your actions demonstrate a sincere desire to welcome and serve in all circumstances. Even when you are in adversarial situations, it is possible to disagree vehemently and still value the other person and treat him or her with honor.

3. **Take a personal interest.** This resonates deep within our souls — to be known by others and treasured for who we

are. If we acknowledge and affirm others' individuality and workplace contributions, we open up the possibility for strong relationships, better business outcomes, and the spread of holy, practical virtue.

4. **Examine your motivation.** The motivation to treat others well has to extend beyond business. The desire to excel in business is good and holy, but our faith calls us to strive for more than just worldly success. We need to excel for Christ and help love others into heaven — a much more comprehensive goal.

5. **Be generous with your time.** One of the ways we can most decisively show our commitment to others is through giving them our time. Just as spouses need to give one another time to nurture a lifetime bond, people with whom we work need our presence to be convinced we care about them as individuals.

❓ QUESTIONS FOR REFLECTION

1. Have you ever known anyone who is using his or her talents to the utmost? Describe the situation.

2. Do you treat others consistently with Christian charity, regardless of the circumstances? What are the impediments to this in your workplace?

3. Does your organizational culture value people? What are some of the qualities manifested as a result?

4. Who has influenced you personally in your career? Did he or she take a personal interest in you, and if so, how?

5. What are the benefits of being generous with time? Is this difficult for you? Why or why not?

Chapter 8

Workplace Witnesses

How to Lead Others to Christ Through Actions, Then Words

"The disciple of Christ must not only keep the faith and live on it, but also profess it, confidently bear witness to it, and spread it."

Catechism of the Catholic Church, 1816

Opus Dei

Opus Dei translates into "work of God," and the organization is — so far — the only personal prelature in the Catholic Church. Think of it as a diocese, with its own bishop, dedicated to a common spirituality but without geographic boundaries. Far from the caricature presented in popular novels, the charism of Opus Dei is simple — it's all about living out the faith by sanctifying our daily work.

I'm not a member, but I have been an admirer of the spirituality of Opus Dei for many years. The founder, St. Josemaría Escrivá, was canonized by Blessed John Paul II in 2002. In the words of the pope, "his life and message have taught countless Christian faithful, particularly laypeople, engaged in the most varied professions, to transform their ordinary work into prayer, service of others, and a path towards holiness" (Decree of Canonization of Saint Josemaría Escrivá).

The key here is transforming work into prayer, and the opportunity to do so is presented to each human being on earth. After all, how else can we "pray without ceasing," as

St. Paul tells us in 1 Thessalonians 5:17? It seems clear that in order to follow this teaching, we must include our work. Compartmentalizing our work just doesn't cut it. Instead, the Gospel invites us to an intense, abiding integration of our lives.

So whether your workplace is a hospital, an office, a forest, my dining room (typically strewn with computers and books), or any of the myriad workplaces found around the world, we each find our fulfillment in the same goal. To the extent we sanctify our work for God, we find true — and enduring — success.

This is why the very definition of success is fundamentally different for us as Christians. We recognize the imperative to go far beyond mere worldly "success" as it is commonly understood. Wealth is fine, but how we achieve it (through ethical means) is more important. Although we don't condemn powerful positions, big salaries, nice houses, or any of the trappings of wealth, they are not our ultimate goal. In fact, these things can (if we become attached to them in a disordered manner) detract from our true success, which is to live a life of heroic virtue and attain the riches of heaven by God's grace, along with as many people as we can bring with us!

Show and Tell

So how do we achieve this in the workplace?

We sure have come a long way on the path to secularization. Many Catholics work in organizations where openly sharing the faith is considered "proselytizing" and viewed in a negative light. Having said that, effective workplace evangelization seldom begins with a coworker being proselytized. Recall the words of Jesus in the Gospel of Mark, "Whoever wishes to come after me must deny himself, take up his cross, and follow me" (Mark 8:34). Here and in many other instances, Jesus demonstrates that authentic conversion is voluntary — a key element of a charitable approach.

One of my favorite quotations, mistakenly attributed to St. Francis of Assisi, is "Preach the Gospel at all times. Use words if necessary." Even though scholars say the actual quote is not from St. Francis, it certainly reflects a Franciscan spirit. The point is directly relevant to today's workplaces — our greatest witness to Christ comes through our actions first, and our words are a distant second.

A friend of mine has been doing this for years. Tim is an executive in a technology-driven company, and he strives to live his faith at work in many practical ways. Despite a hectic schedule, he seldom misses daily Mass, even when he's extremely busy. He approaches his tasks with intensity and perseverance. His treatment of others is firm yet charitable. And here's a particularly endearing factor: his humility is marked by a daily prayer that he be successful and never know it. His dedication to personal sanctity is exemplary.

Tim doesn't hide his faith, although he doesn't take an aggressive approach either. His colleagues know that he's Catholic, but even those who want nothing to do with Christianity respect Tim. His work reflects a good use of personal talents, applied for the benefit of others, consistently each day. This has sowed many seeds throughout his workplace based on positive example. These are seeds the Holy Spirit can cause to grow.

Another friend is slightly more overt in her approach. She has ten children, and she keeps pictures of the family on her desk. Bobbie is deeply intellectual and enthusiastic, and people like being around her due to her joyful personality. But ask her about the children or why she and her husband have so many, and she'll tell you straight. You might even leave with a copy of *Humanae Vitae*, Pope Paul VI's landmark encyclical regarding artificial contraception. Bobbie uses a combination of who she is, manifested by her actions, and follows up with cheerful, nonjudgmental explanations.

Home Work

Like Bobbie, recall my wife Kathi's decisive gift of self that resulted in our eight children. This act of generosity to God and me is a modern anomaly — people think we're nuts. The witness of children is met with various responses, including admiration, skepticism, or sometimes, outright derision. Yet it remains a challenge to non-Catholics who, when confronted with this reality, ask a simple question: Why?

When this happens, we need to be prepared to defend our faith charitably, and to explain the reasons we engage in such "nutty" behavior. At the same time, we need to do so in the spirit of Jesus' invitation. We can always have confidence in the Holy Spirit's ability to soften hearts to be receptive to the Gospel. Our job is not to force the truth on people, much less to do so on the spot. Conversion of heart is more often a process of seeds being planted than a single, dramatic event. Trust God and pray. Think about it: if He could convert St. Paul, He can handle your coworker.

But what if your work *is* the home? For those who don't think that being a domestic engineer is work, just visit my house. Kathi's workplace is challenging (some might even call it a hostile environment at times!), and the rewards are *loooong* term. She works crazy hours, deals with unreasonable "client" demands, and has to deal with extraordinary levels of conflict. The paycheck is terrible, there aren't many employee benefits, and if she's really successful, the kids leave!

I am a firm proponent of homemaking being serious work. Female or male, mom or dad, it doesn't matter. If that's your job, you have your hands full and wear a lot of hats. Facilities, finance, human resources, procurement, operations — it's all you, baby. Given this overwhelming responsibility, how can we not only keep our heads above water but also live up to our calling to spread the faith?

Perhaps Kathi is an unfair example, since I'm so completely and unabashedly biased. But the first thing she did right was saying yes to God with our mutual fertility, and then she followed through on that commitment, one day at a time, with love and perseverance. What better way to spread the faith than to transmit it to children, "the supreme gift of marriage" (*Gaudium et Spes*, Pastoral Constitution on the Church in the Modern World, 50)? Not only this, but I can't tell you how many times the mere fact that we have eight children in today's culture is a witness in itself.

Workplace Wonder

I have had the pleasure of working with other Catholics in the workplace who have impressed me with the witness they bring in ways consistent with their individual gifts. For example, I know a woman named Ann who is one of the most cheerful individuals on the planet. The joy she brings to her work every day inspires everyone she meets.

Part of the reason this resonates is because the workplace deals out its share of emotional downers. Dealing with a cranky customer, experiencing conflict with a colleague, or receiving a poor performance review generally triggers negative emotions — and so, resilient, cheerful personalities like Ann's are attractive. She always helps people feel just a little more positive, often just the ticket after absorbing some negative input. Ann helps her coworkers maintain perspective through her encouraging, positive demeanor. She's a real gift.

Another friend of mine, Greg, is always willing to help others, but in a different way. He has a "heart of service" to which others are instinctively drawn. Especially when he provides help to others who are experiencing difficulty, the gratitude that results is inspiring; he has a real knack for being in the right place at the right time and offering his help. Such acts of generosity and kindness are capable of softening hearts and attuning ears to the voice of Christ. After all, part of the reason God gave us these gifts is to use them to draw others toward Him.

In Greg's case, he goes out of his way to help people out with those silly, yet confounding computer problems we all seem to experience from time to time. His service corresponds to his natural aptitude for computers. So he becomes a "go-to" guy for folks all over the office, and his colleagues genuinely appreciate his help. Yet another reason people like him so much is the fact that he's a great listener. He doesn't try to solve every problem (just computer ones), but by listening, he demonstrates his caring.

Ann and Greg both use their individual gifts — Ann, beginning with her cheerful personality, and Greg, beginning with his computer skills and communication abilities. Both sets of gifts can be equally effective means of planting seeds in the hearts of others. The point is that we can all use our gifts at work not only for business purposes — although that's certainly a good thing — but also to plant seeds of the Gospel.

Distinctive Differences

When we love God and seek to serve others, we need to have the courage to be different. Think of the simile of salt: "Salt is good, but if salt itself loses its taste, with what can its flavor be restored?" (Luke 14:34). We are called to be "salt of the earth" in a way that enriches others.

One of my favorite ways to provoke an incredulous response in the workplace is to speak positively about my wife. It is always sincere, since I am completely crazy about her. After all, she must be pretty special to have eight children with me! However, in my experience, most people are much more accustomed to hearing negative messages in the workplace regarding marriage and spouses. When telling people how much I love Kathi, the reaction is almost always amazement, often followed by appreciation.

As Catholics, we know marriage as a sacrament, worthy of great esteem and admiration. Therefore, to honor our spouses is (or should be) a natural inclination. Since this is not the norm, it is for us an extraordinary opportunity. Most people want to believe in marriage, and we can encourage them to do so in a way that is positive and uplifting.

At the end of the day, we all have the ability to spread the Gospel in a way that is just as unique as we are. Some are more direct, and others are quiet. Some are scholarly, and some are simple. The goal is to use our gifts to the utmost out of love for our Lord and for the benefit of others. After all, if we truly love others in the way Christ described, don't we want them to spend eternity in the presence of God? Just as we spend hours planning our upcoming sales presentation or business plan, how much more ingenious should we be in pointing others to Christ?

ACTION STEPS

In order to effectively share — not force — the Gospel, we need to think beyond our preconceived notions and consider the following:

1. **Work on yourself first.** Work first on yourself and who you are becoming. The starting point for a credible witness is the quiet inward process in which we seek to be transformed to more fully reflect our Lord. Strive for perfection and persevere, even when you don't achieve it. Begin anew each day.

2. **Sanctify your work.** Each day's work is an opportunity to transform our natural efforts into a source of supernatural

worship. God wants to be Lord of our entire lives, including our work. By offering each day's work for His glory, praying about work issues, and doing our work for God first, we draw closer to Him and inspire others.

3. **Use actions before words.** Always keep in mind that actions speak louder than words. Our credibility increases if we are seen as modeling the behavior and attitudes we recommend to others. Consistency in action also opens the hearts of others to be receptive to words that reflect God's love.

4. **Use your gifts.** You can share the Gospel in a way that is unique to you. Take the gifts God has given you and use them. When you do your work with a spirit of love (which encompasses excellence and honoring others), you lead others to Christ.

5. **Tell your story.** Our faith is transformative, and when it changes us, there's a story to tell. Since we all yearn for a better life, stories of transformation resonate deep within the human heart. The greatest witness is to be thoroughly converted to the Gospel ourselves.

? QUESTIONS FOR REFLECTION

1. Have you ever attempted to talk to someone in your workplace about your faith? How did it go?

2. Do you know any Catholics who provide an outstanding example of living their faith at work? How is this manifested in practical terms?

3. Is the concept of sanctifying work something that makes sense to you? Why or why not?

4. Do you think action is more effective than talking to someone when it comes to evangelization? What are the impediments to evangelization in your work?

5. What approach would make sense for you to encourage others to seek Christ, given your particular gifts and talents?

Chapter 9

You Don't Drink Diet Coke?

How to Handle Diversity in the Workplace by Recognizing That We're All God's Children

"All men are called to the same end: God himself. There is a certain resemblance between the union of the divine persons and the fraternity that men are to establish among themselves in truth and love. Love of neighbor is inseparable from love for God."

Catechism of the Catholic Church, 1878

Variety — the Spice of Life

One of the advantages of my youth was exposure to people from all over the world. Early on, my dad taught an international business program, and we had students from various countries over at our house on a regular basis. During high school, I went to a boarding school and had roommates and friends from places such as Nigeria, Hong Kong, South America, Iran, and the Caribbean.

When I started my career at Sony, I had the opportunity to work with a similarly diverse group. Many of my bosses and coworkers were from Japan, of course, but there were others from India, England, China, and even Kuwait. My studies at Franciscan University continued this trend, as there were students from countries around the globe in attendance. One of my good friends was from Nepal. Of course, I was an international student myself!

My friends from such diverse cultural backgrounds also held widely varying religious beliefs. I was exposed not only to many Christian denominations but also Buddhism, Hinduism, Judaism, atheism, etc.

In many ways, this upbringing laid the foundation for embracing Catholicism as an adult. As part of a pluralistic culture, despite being enriched by the history and traditions of those surrounding me, I thirsted for objective truth.

The Same, Only Different

When I was baptized and became Catholic, all the desires of my heart for truth were fulfilled. The night was utterly transformative — Baptism, Confirmation, and First Communion at Easter Vigil.

Among the many attractive elements that drew me to Catholicism, one was that the faith transcends nation, race, and color. Its universality is a source of beauty: since Jesus Himself is truth, and truth is immutable, the reflection of Christ in the Church's teachings on matters of faith and morals is utterly compelling. Doctrinal consistency with natural law, extraordinarily well-articulated expositions of the faith (such as St. Augustine or St. Thomas Aquinas), and sacramental grace on top of it all? It's awesome!

Truth resonates within all human hearts, no matter who they are or where they're from. Not everyone will accept it, of course, but for all the efforts aimed at calling right wrong and wrong right, God calls everyone to Himself — sometimes quietly and gently, but persistently. I also know that prayer works. I've seen it happen time and time again.

Given that foundation, the faithful have good reason to be confident in the Church's teachings. Although we have tremendous diversity in national origins, appearances, skills, beliefs, ways of thinking, and favorite flavors of ice cream, we all share a common purpose: to know God, to love Him, and to serve Him. We're the same, only different. Created in the image of God Himself, our diversity reflects a sublime reality of the divine will. So diversity is great, right?

Diversity Training

In the workplace, the word "diversity" is sometimes reflective of a worldly ideology rather than the divine will. Of course, some of the aims of this movement are positive and seek to honor people and facilitate communication, mutual respect, and other worthy outcomes. I like approaching business problems with diverse disciplines, skill sets, and ways of thinking at the table — in my experience, this leads to better decisions. However, in some cases "diversity" efforts seek to legitimize a relativistic moral worldview that can be at odds with the Church's teachings.

For example, one hot diversity topic is homosexuality in the workplace. It's an emotionally charged and sometimes contentious issue. There has been heated rhetoric on both sides of the debate, along with name-calling and even outright hostility. Many people, including some Christians, regard homosexuality as morally evil. On the other hand, some consider it a fundamental human right and morally acceptable.

Happily, the Church's teaching on the matter is not only crystal clear, but it also provides practical guidance for daily living. The Congregation for the Doctrine of the Faith, echoed by the *Catechism of the Catholic Church*, states that "homosexual acts are intrinsically disordered" (CCC 2357). So the moral judgment of the Church is definitive, and it delineates clearly that it opposes homosexual *acts*, not homosexual persons. This is a critical distinction.

The *Catechism* goes on to state, "They [homosexual persons — those with "deep-seated homosexual tendencies"] must be accepted with respect, compassion, and sensitivity. Every sign

of unjust discrimination in their regard should be avoided. . . .
Homosexual persons are called to chastity" (CCC 2358-2359).
So in essence, we aren't called to be alike; we're called to honor
everyone. We're all children of God.

"I Have a Domestic Partner"

My first exposure to this type of "diversity" in the workplace
occurred many years ago. My company had just hired a very
bright individual — great credentials, relevant experience, per-
sonable. His name was Jeff.

On his first day, we exchanged the usual pleasantries, and
he asked about my family and children (I was fairly notori-
ous as the crazy guy with a bunch of kids). When I returned
the question, he paused for a second and said: "Well, I have
a domestic partner." I was shocked. Call me naïve, but I just
didn't see that one coming.

So for the next few days, Jeff was very much on my mind.
I liked him but had never worked this closely with a gay man.
I spent much time in prayer, read Catholic documents dealing
with the subject, and sought spiritual direction. I wanted to
make sure my treatment of Jeff was appropriate, not only in the
eyes of my employer but also in the eyes of the Church.

Now, I was familiar with the issue. Canada grappled with
the topic for many years, and now allows same-sex "marriage."
Support for this ideology runs deep in the culture, and dissent
isn't well tolerated (somewhat ironic). In fact, certain biblical
passages condemning homosexual acts are regarded as hate
speech and can't be broadcast on television or radio.

So I had already heard plenty of arguments on both sides
of the issue, including from human resources as well as from
political and religious perspectives. That's not what I was after.
I wanted to figure out how to best relate to Jeff. As it turns out,

I didn't have to look very far. Jesus' own example provides great practical guidance.

The Love of a Friend

Jesus spent a lot of time on earth with sinners, and this fact jumped out at me. Not only was I acutely conscious of my own sinfulness, but I was also grateful and enthusiastic about the faith I had discovered. In some ways, I felt like the woman in the Gospel of Luke (7:36-50) who wept at Jesus' feet and was so thankful to have been forgiven. Being around other sinners doesn't bother me — we're all in good company with one another.

In all aspects of life, we're called to strive for the salvation of souls, both our own and others. Sexual sin is pervasive in our culture, and simply deeming it acceptable doesn't help anyone. I have often worked with people who are cohabiting, despite solid research suggesting that this is a poor substitute or precursor for marriage. In the case of both my cohabiting and gay friends, Catholic beliefs don't line up with their actions. So what's a good Catholic to do?

The answer is to imitate Christ. Jesus loved everyone He met, and He demonstrated this love through friendship. The workplace affords us an outstanding opportunity to *be* friends to others — in the case of homosexual persons (and everyone else), this means treating them with profound respect. If we are to be truly Christian in our approach, we should offer friendship without reservation, along with an appreciation for the individual's particular gifts, skills, and accomplishments.

We also need to resist thinking that confrontation in the workplace is an effective tool of evangelization. A more positive approach is to listen first, and then to watch for opportunities to share the faith in a way that responds to the needs of the individual. Should discussions arise, consider setting ground rules at the outset: "Before discussing this, let's agree that no matter what our opinions are, we'll be respectful toward each other." As we hear in Scripture: "Always be ready to give an explanation to anyone who asks you for a reason for your hope, but do it with gentleness and reverence . . ." (1 Peter 3:15-16).

Our goal in the workplace should be to first live a life worthy of the Gospel, and to pray for others, including those with whom we disagree. The Church has consistently taught that homosexual acts are sinful, and simultaneously, that we are loved regardless of sexual orientation or behavior. Whether our gay friends agree with this or not, we're called to reflect Christ's love and offer our friendship.

Finally, we know the value of offering sacrifices for the benefit of others — Masses, fasting, Holy Hours, novenas, and so on. These are all opportunities for us to grow closer to our Lord, while simultaneously drawing souls closer to Him. Pray for those who oppose the Church's teachings, and don't be surprised when they do oppose them: Jesus warned us, after all. God will lead us through even the most complicated situations.

Joseph Who?

Early in my career, I worked with individuals from various faith traditions. This provided further opportunities for my personal learning and growth. Some individuals were highly critical of Catholicism (including a number of ex-Catholics), and others were fervent in their own beliefs. One colleague was Mormon and liked to talk about it.

Jamie came into a meeting one day, and as it happened, the other participants had just raided the refrigerator and found that we only had Diet Coke. Nothing else — no water, juice, or other kinds of soft drinks. So everyone grabbed a can and sat down. Everyone except Jamie.

"What's the matter, Jamie? You don't drink Diet Coke?" someone asked.

"As a matter of fact, I don't," Jamie replied with a broad smile. Then it all started tumbling out. "The idea is to avoid addiction, which is why Mormons generally avoid caffeine. You see, back in the 1800s, Joseph Smith . . ."

"Joseph who?"

"You know, Joseph Smith, prophet and founder of the Church of Latter Day Saints."

"Oh."

A lively discussion ensued about some of the distinctive characteristics of Mormonism and differences between Mormon beliefs and those of others in the room. It took up the first few minutes of the meeting, but I just sat back and listened. It helped me to understand Jamie.

Back to Basics

In so many ways, dealing with those of other religions in the workplace is an opportunity. I'm consistently impressed by the depth of respect people of other faiths have for the Catholic Church. There is often common ground — although again, we are not called to agree. Knowing someone else is deeply committed to his or her (different) faith doesn't lessen my enthusiasm about Catholicism one iota. If nothing else, we should all share a desire for religious freedom, a hallmark of a truly free society.

So with Jamie, I found that his clean living and personal discipline were admirable attributes. In fact, he sometimes challenged me to "up my game," so to speak. Although we disagreed on many key issues, we treated one another with respect and a spirit of friendship. As it happened, this was also true of my gay colleague Jeff.

By Whose Authority?

As a child, I was taught to respect authority, and my conversion experience to Catholicism enhanced this understanding further. So when I first came up against a situation where the authority at work was opposed to my faith, it caused me great consternation.

My company decided that it wanted 100 percent participation in its annual charitable campaign. All employees were, well, *encouraged* to participate. We were even given incentives to contribute a certain percentage of our salaries.

Unfortunately, at the time, the list of beneficiaries included abortion providers.

Some saw this as no big deal, since the list also included several Catholic organizations. Although this was true, at the time it was still very troubling for me. I wanted to be perceived as a team player within the firm and to respect the authority of those who provided me with a livelihood, but at the same time I had no interest in funding abortions.

So I prayed. Specifically, I asked the Holy Spirit to provide a solution to the problem. Within a week, I discovered a (new, at that time) program to direct my contribution specifically to the local Catholic organizations. Voilà! Problem solved.

Get Creative

Of course, not all problems we run into in the workplace are so easily resolved — some aren't, *ever*. Yet we still have the tools of our faith available to help in our time of need. Prayer is always the first step, with prayers for wisdom to the Holy Spirit being a favorite of mine. I have been amazed at how many times this has resulted in a creative third option, when initially it appeared that it had to be either A or B, both problematic. That's the beauty of praying for wisdom: God is able to see what we can't, and can lead us in the right direction even when we are completely in the dark.

Even when the authority within our organizations is off the mark (such as companies directly sponsoring Planned Parenthood) relative to our faith, there is still an opportunity for us to act as the catalyst for positive change. Besides having due respect for authority, we can pray that even our objections are made in a spirit of love, with gentleness and wisdom.

In other words, it's not just what we do; it's how we do it. There are times that Jesus called the Pharisees hypocrites, and others when He gently told people to get their priorities in order (for example, the rich man in Mark 10:17-31). There is no single, simple approach — which is why we need God's guidance every step of the way.

ACTION STEPS

In order to speak the truth in love at work, consider these ideas:

1. **Recognize that we're all children of God.** There is intrinsic value in all people, regardless of the decisions they make in life. Think of the Catholic pro-life perspective that "all life is sacred," and apply it to your coworkers.

2. **Speak the truth in love.** Although we can never waffle on the truth in matters of faith and morals, how we say things is often just as important as what we're saying. There is no dichotomy here. Truth and love are not opposed; they're both personified in Jesus Himself.

3. **Find common ground.** People are attracted to Catholicism when they see Catholics living what we believe and treating others with love. We can always find common ground

with others, and this can serve as the basis for the strong
relationships to which we are called by Jesus.

4. **Look for creative solutions.** With the help of the Holy
   Spirit, seek win-win solutions at a higher level — be mind-
   ful of the spiritual impact of your actions at work, in addition to their practical value. When in doubt, seek spiritual
   direction — and for a spiritually supercharged effect, pray
   the Rosary.

5. **Honor authority.** Sometimes being right isn't the only
   thing that matters. We also need to honor legitimate authority and use even our objections as opportunities for
   individual conversion (including our own!).

 ## QUESTIONS FOR REFLECTION

1. Do you often feel like a child of God? Do you have trouble
   viewing others in this way?

2. Describe a time when you had to speak the truth in love in
   the workplace. What was the result?

3. What has your experience been with diversity in the workplace? Have you ever had your faith challenged?

4. Have you ever experienced God's guidance in work situations in ways that go beyond your own wisdom, when it
   seemed like your actions were divinely guided? What happened?

5. Describe the atmosphere in your workplace as it pertains
   to your religious beliefs. Has this ever caused any problems
   for you? If so, how?

Chapter 10

Call in the Consultants

How to Maintain Perspective Through Spiritual Direction and Workplace Mentors

"Good teacher, what must I do to inherit eternal life?"
Mark 10:17

Timing Is Everything

Hannah was a high-level executive in a bank. After almost thirty years, she had gone through several mergers, restructurings, and management shake-ups. With a strong work ethic, impeccable credentials, and a long record of success in her business unit, she had survived every threat to her career. It was the only job she ever had. Until now.

Hannah's bank was facing a layoff of unprecedented proportions. Almost 20 percent of the workforce was being eliminated, and Hannah was on the list.

Shortly after the announcement, Hannah was at home trying to absorb the news when the phone rang. She answered to the sound of a familiar voice. "Hello, Hannah? It's Maria. How are you?" Maria was a longtime friend of Hannah's, an attorney by training and recently retired in her early sixties. "Oh, Maria, not so good." The story poured out, along with Hannah's fears and disappointments. "I have no idea what I'll do. But I'm so glad you called!"

Can You Negotiate?

Fortunately for Hannah, Maria encouraged her to negotiate certain aspects of the severance agreement. She asked questions that helped Hannah to see beyond the immediate situation, and she offered reassurance to salve her insecurities. By the end of their conversation, Hannah had scribbled several notes and had formed a plan in her mind as to how she should proceed.

The next day, Hannah's prayer time included thanksgiving for her good friend, and prayers for wisdom in dealing with the discussion she was to have with the human resources (HR) department that day.

As it turned out, there was room for negotiation, and by following Maria's advice, Hannah was able to improve her severance package. In retrospect, the timing of the call couldn't have been better. Perhaps due to Maria's legal training, or her sincere empathy and desire to help, many of the points they had discussed were directly relevant to the negotiation. That phone call had been very valuable.

God works through everyday, mundane experiences such as a random phone call. Maria acted as an instrument of God's grace, as we all do when we live in His will — often without even recognizing it. When we abandon ourselves to the divine will, life takes on a spirit of adventure, as we seek to please our Lord.

Spiritual GPS

Have you ever noticed how difficult it can be to maintain perspective when you're going through difficulties at work? This is one of the reasons the insight of others is so important. When we're confused, overwhelmed, or doubtful about our own talents or abilities, they offer something we don't have: objectivity.

Have you ever heard of God speaking through others? My wife insists that the Holy Spirit speaks through her frequently! So prayers can sometimes result in answers that are verbally provided . . . from sources as close as the next cubicle or the nearest parish. At work, we generally call people who serve in this capacity mentors — whether formal or informal. In the case of priests or certain others with the requisite training, they can be spiritual directors. Both mentors and spiritual directors offer us an invaluable service. Through their knowledge of us, including that of our work and spiritual lives, they provide us objectivity spoken in love — sometimes tough love. It's a beautiful thing.

As a young man, I used to pray to God for forgiveness or ask for His intervention in situations, and I knew He listened. Upon becoming Catholic, one of the unexpected joys of confession was hearing — audibly — another human being acting *in persona Christi* ("in the person of Christ"). Spiritual direction is much the same, where a mentor or priest is able to offer verbal advice, given our particular circumstances. Such input is a true gift.

You're Fired

Of all the duties I have carried out in the corporate world, the one I have struggled with most is firing people. Although I believe it is justified and necessary at times, it can also be difficult to reconcile with placing a high value on the individual.

At one point, due to a corporate consolidation, I had to "synergize" (fire) a number of coworkers within the space of a couple hours. Anticipating the event was emotionally draining; many of the individuals were friends, and I had hired some of them myself. Prior to the big day, I sought spiritual direction.

Father Joseph was gracious and understanding, as usual. He asked a number of good questions and had me explain the situation thoroughly before attempting any recommendations. "Given the situation, it appears that you don't have much discretion over the names on the list. Is that true?" Unfortunately, it was. I had been given the opportunity to provide input, but with certain functions being clearly redundant in the consolidated entity, I didn't have much to go on.

As I explained to Father Joseph, I had made a strong appeal on behalf of one individual where the redundancy wasn't quite so clear, but to no avail. "Yes, Father . . . if I push any harder, it probably won't help, and I may lose credibility. That could put my own family at risk and reduce my chances of helping those who are staying at the company."

We discussed various other details, and Father Joseph, in his wisdom, gave me several pointers for honoring the people affected, doing my best as steward for the company, and helping everyone to get past the immediate crisis. He promised to pray for me, along with the others impacted.

In addition, I spoke with a good friend, Larry, who had a great HR background and recommended a particular article on managers handling downsizing properly by treating people with dignity. As it turned out, it was extremely helpful. Although the day was one of the most difficult in my career, there was also grace that resulted from the wise input of both Father Joseph and Larry.

Big Decisions, Small Decisions

Several years ago, I was considering a career move. There were a number of conflicting factors, including not only career but also family and personal considerations. My mind was racing during the process, to the point where I became thoroughly frustrated and overwhelmed. In this case, I decided to take a step back and write down my approach, including a prioritized list of whom to consult.

First on the list was God! In fact, "praying through" decisions has become a way of life. Some people wonder whether it's right to pray about business issues. I have long had the sense that God wants us to pray to Him about everything — big things, small things, and in-between things. Our work is a big part of our daily life — how could we exclude it in our prayer time and remain faithful in *all things*? God's love is so all-encompassing, and it's comforting to know that He is willing to listen to all of our concerns, even if it requires a keen divine sense of humor!

Next on the list was my wife. The vocation to marriage provides couples with such a deep, intimate relationship that it is afforded the marvelous honor of being a sacrament! As a result, our spouses know us like no other — both strengths and weaknesses. If our motivation is wrong (we're going after a job primarily for money, but we'll be miserable, for example), our spouse will see it first.

I'm also a big fan of formal spiritual direction with a priest. This provides two huge benefits. First, we're able to participate in sacramental confession, often useful during times of uncertainty or struggle. Second, priests who are good spiritual directors have the ability to guide us with objectivity and ask questions that consider the broader circumstances of our lives, including our faith.

Finally, I have a network of trusted family and friends who know me well and are happy to provide advice. My dad is at the top of this list, and I also have a couple close friends, such as my mentor Joe, who are wonderful resources. One of the key elements in selecting individuals for this list is their ability to challenge me, not simply agree with everything I say. Positive reinforcement is great, but being asked tough questions in a loving way is critical in achieving the purpose of faithful and prudent decision-making.

Be the Miracle

Sometimes, the shoe is on the other foot, so to speak, and we are called upon to advise others. In such cases, the first thing to remember is to listen before we speak. Of course, the most powerful thing we can do is pray on their behalf. Through our intercessory prayers and acts of service and penance for others, we tap into the source of all wisdom.

We also need to have the humility to listen and ask more questions than provide answers. Often what our coworkers need is an empathetic ear, more than advice. When your sentences all begin with "This is what you need to do . . ." then this is what *you* need to do: stop. Listen, seek to understand, and ask questions reflecting that you're listening. Your coworkers will appreciate your input even more than if you offer stellar wisdom. Strange but true. Try it.

Another key is simply showing up. Sometimes, the best thing we can do is simply be there for the other person, offering support and a place to safely unload their emotions. A solution isn't always the solution; sometimes the process is designed to help the individual grow.

ACTION STEPS

To enjoy the benefits of spiritual direction and reflect the wisdom of Christ for others, try the following:

1. **Look for God in the little things.** Just like Hannah, we can look for God in the regular events of everyday life. Some might view the timing of Maria's call as mere coincidence, but Hannah knew better. God sometimes works in dramatic ways, but more often we can sense His presence in ordinary, mundane events.

2. **Think long-term.** If our faith is real, we should have a much longer perspective than most — it should include eternity. Often the most difficult circumstances are for our long-term benefit (such as Hannah's sorrowful departure from the bank that turned into the joy of her second career) and to keep us on the path to heaven.

3. **Seek out spiritual direction.** Spiritual direction brings the perspective of eternal wisdom, where we apply our faith to our daily work with the benefit of objectivity. As human beings, emotion can sometimes cloud our judgment, and spiritual directors or faithful friends can often be "angels" (messengers of the Lord) that He uses for our benefit and that of others.

4. **Pray about everything.** Persistent prayer works. Good times, bad times, we can't always change circumstances, but we can always be faithful.

5. **Be there for others.** Although we may not feel like angels for others, take comfort in the fact that God is able to use even imperfect instruments like us to accomplish great things. Our work provides a wonderful opportunity to love others simply by being there for them.

❓ QUESTIONS FOR REFLECTION

1. Have you ever experienced a "coincidental" event at work that, in retrospect, you believe was God's divine intervention? What happened?

2. Describe a time when something difficult happened in your work and an eternal perspective changed the way you looked at the situation.

3. Do you seek out spiritual direction and the counsel of faithful friends on a regular basis? How has this helped you in your work?

4. Have you ever prayed for something with tremendous persistence, just to have your prayers granted? What about times your prayers have not been granted? Give examples.

5. Describe a time you were there at the right time for an individual or event. How did this affect the situation?

Chapter 11

"Forgive Us Our Trespasses"

How to Overcome Interpersonal Strife at Work Through Forgiveness

> *"If we really want to love, we must learn to forgive."*
>
> Blessed Mother Teresa of Calcutta

Of Course I Forgive You!

Toward the end of my undergraduate days at Franciscan University, I had a conversation with a good friend that always stuck with me. Peter was a theology major, a brilliant guy with a great sense of humor who planned to pursue graduate studies in theology (he eventually earned his Ph.D. in the subject). Kathi and I, along with Peter and his girlfriend Naomi, got together every now and then for dinner and some friendly conversation. As a business student, I was always interested in Peter's views on the application of theological principles to business.

On this particular evening, the topic of forgiveness came up. Peter and I became absorbed and carried on an energetic discussion about the spiritual value of forgiveness, much to the ladies' disbelief. At the time, we thought the frequent exclamations and gasps we heard in the background might have been admiration for our keen spiritual insights. However, after dinner Kathi and Naomi were happy to inform us that our theoretical command of the topic far exceeded our personal application.

Undaunted, Peter and I came to a somewhat radical conclusion that night: if we truly understood the value of forgiveness, we would be thrilled when there was an opportunity to forgive someone. This recognizes the incredible value of being merciful, knowing that God's mercy so far exceeds our own. Even when we considered the question from the perspective of a business environment, we agreed that the principle still held true. It sounds crazy, I know.

But is it really crazy? Or is it merely countercultural? Jesus speaks about forgiveness frequently in the Gospels, with perhaps the most famous being a line in the Lord's Prayer: ". . . and forgive us our debts, / as we forgive our debtors" (Matthew 6:12). In Luke's Gospel, Jesus again speaks clearly on the subject: "If your brother sins, rebuke him; and if he repents, forgive him. And if he wrongs you seven times in one day and returns to you seven times saying, 'I am sorry,' you should forgive him" (Luke 17:3-4).

What could someone possibly do to us that would be so egregious that we would rather not forgive him and risk God treating us in the same way?

Beyond Egregious

Years later, I was shocked to hear of the murder of two Franciscan University students, Aaron Land and Brian Muha. Equally shocking, before the bodies were even discovered, Brian's mother, Rachel, had come forward to publicly forgive the young men who killed her son. As a parent, I can't imagine a more traumatic or egregious set of circumstances. The emotional and physical impact of this crime on Rachel must have been staggering. This story has served as a model of forgiveness in my mind ever since. Forgiveness isn't just an emotion, it isn't complete when you feel a sense of peace about it, and it's not only valid after the fact. Forgiveness is a function of grace, an act of the will, and a process that requires standing by the decision as it's revisited.

Through Rachel's forgiveness, grace flowed. She has since founded the "Run the Race Club," and other programs as part of the Brian Muha Memorial Foundation, which serves inner-city youth. The club's motto is "Turning Tragedy into Hope." So through a senseless and brutal murder, God brought about extraordinary good. With Rachel as His instrument, countless people have been impacted by Brian's story — and Rachel's. Consider the witness this has provided over the many years since Brian's death. Now, most of the conflicts that require forgiveness in our daily lives are relatively minor, but they still offer us an opportunity to draw closer to our Lord. Especially at work.

Forgive, Me?

Why is forgiveness so often necessary in the workplace?

Perhaps it's the pressures of today's workplace, which are often acute. Businesses find themselves in an unprecedented era of global competition. Nonprofit organizations face funding reductions, and governments are in a state of fiscal crisis. Productivity demands are high, the rate of change is swift, and workers are frequently stressed out.

On top of all that, we have to work with one another. Of all the issues that I have dealt with in my career, the most difficult ones involve interpersonal strife. The source could be a chatty coworker, a difficult customer, a supplier who breaks a promise, or a boss whose demands are unreasonable.

People at work are often under pressure. Have you ever noticed that people under pressure act differently? Maybe it manifests itself through a short fuse before a fiery temper erupts, or impatience, or lack of empathy. It could even trigger dishonest behavior from an otherwise trustworthy individual.

So with all the potentially incendiary ingredients in the workplace, if you're looking for opportunities to forgive people, you're in the right place.

A Key to Success

No matter what your occupation, relationships are a key to success. And forgiveness is a key to building and sustaining relationships. As we require forgiveness from God for our relationship with Him to thrive, we need to forgive others, and to be forgiven. When this happens, our relationships become characterized by trust, one of the most critical elements for effective teamwork. So did the conclusion Peter and I reached as students about the importance of forgiveness stand the test of time and experience in the real world?

I remember a situation playing out between two colleagues many years ago named Jessica and Andrea. The two were good friends, and they often helped each other out on projects at the office, even though they were in different departments. Jessica was energetic and outgoing, while Andrea tended to be quiet and intellectual. With complementary skill sets, they made a great team.

Unfortunately, Jessica had some problems at home that began to impact her ability to function. Although I wasn't aware of any details, I had heard that her husband was divorcing her and dating someone else. The situation was clearly taking its toll on Jessica, and even her friendship with Andrea began to suffer. With emotions running high and a deadline looming on one of Jessica's big projects, a bitter argument erupted one day. Apparently, one of Jessica's other coworkers knew some details regarding the divorce that Jessica believed could only have come from Andrea.

From that day forward, the relationship went straight downhill. Snide remarks were exchanged in meetings in front of others. Derogatory observations were made to other colleagues about the other's weaknesses. Although neither Jessica nor Andrea would admit it publicly, they both felt angry, betrayed, and humiliated.

Why Should I Forgive You?

The relationship remained toxic for well over a year. Meanwhile, Jessica's divorce was finalized, and she was given a huge project that could lead to a highly coveted promotion — and a much-needed salary increase, given her divorce. The only problem was that in the past, Andrea had always helped her with the technical details. Jessica decided it was time to swallow her pride and talk to Andrea.

As you might imagine, Andrea was indignant at first. Jessica tended to be popular, and some of the things she had said to others about Andrea weren't true and had really hurt. At first, Andrea was reluctant to forgive her. At the same time, Andrea missed their relationship, and enough time had passed that some of her anger had dissipated. She wanted her friend back.

Andrea decided to take a chance and forgive Jessica.

Happily, the situation worked out nicely in the long run. Although it took time to rebuild a mutual sense of trust, Andrea did help Jessica with her project, and it led to the promotion. Jessica was so grateful to Andrea for helping her that she reciprocated later and earned Andrea a new position in her department too. The process took almost two years to play out, but in the end Jessica, Andrea, their coworkers, and their company benefitted from their mutual forgiveness. The value of forgiveness went beyond the two people directly involved. It was a powerful testament to the need — and the practical result — of forgiveness.

What's Your Motive?

One of the main obstacles to forgiveness in the workplace is our tendency to "read" motives into others' behavior. This tends to exacerbate conflict and often makes forgiveness more difficult.

I remember giving an extemporaneous speech in a meeting one day and accidentally mangling a sentence. I was attempting to give credit for a great idea to a staff member and meant to say, "Julie had a great idea. For the first time ever, we put email addresses on this brochure."

Instead, here's what came out: "For the first time ever, Julie had a great idea. We put email addresses on this brochure."

Oops.

Besides being completely embarrassed, I had done precisely the opposite of what I intended. Fortunately, most of the people in the audience knew me well enough to give me the benefit of the doubt and assume positive motives. But what about others, who either didn't know me at all or had a more negative perception of me? Could this result in a different conclusion?

You better believe it. Here's the problem. When individuals work with one another, viewing a coworker through a particular "lens" or set of assumptions can result in a self-reinforcing bias. Thankfully, I came through this little gaffe largely unscathed, after several apologies to Julie in front of the group.

What Are They Thinking?

But does it always work out for the best? Consider the following: let's say an employee goes home early one day. No big deal, right? But watch out.

One of his colleagues, who had witnessed the employee being very tired a week prior, might assume the early departure is due to laziness. Another colleague, upon seeing the exact same early departure, might assume the employee is off to another business meeting late in the day and come to the opposite conclusion. Of course, the real reason might be that the employee's spouse was ill that day — invalidating both conclusions!

The problem — and opportunity — is that our beliefs drive our behaviors. However, despite our efforts to "read" other people, the fact is that we don't always do a good job, even with people we know well. So reading into someone else's motives can cause us great consternation at work, since it may lead to a course of action based on false assumptions.

A Christian Approach

Forgiveness can be helpful in these situations as well.

Think about how colleagues with good relationships give one another the benefit of the doubt, as people generally do in trusting relationships. If your good friend at work did something that appeared very unusual, you would probably reserve judgment and ask her about it, right? In a sense, this is *preemptive* forgiveness — a disposition to assume positively.

Given our faith, we know who can be trusted all the time: God Himself. When it comes to judging motives, it's better to leave such matters to God. So even when others truly have negative motives, to the extent we can train ourselves to give them the benefit of the doubt, and offer up their actions and attitudes to God, this helps us to forgive them.

Divining motives in others is a dangerous practice, particularly in a work environment when people are so often under pressure. The right motives to examine are our own. This is one way we can purify ourselves spiritually on a daily basis, learning to detest our own sins more than those of our coworkers.

Grace at Work

Most conflicts in the workplace are relatively minor, and certainly nothing compared to what Rachel Muha experienced. I like to remember her story, since it reminds me that if Rachel could forgive her son's murderers, I should be able to forgive some relatively minor workplace quibble. But as my friend Peter and I speculated so many years ago, forgiveness truly is a powerful tool.

In order to improve in the area of forgiveness, it's best to start small. The workplace offers the opportunity to forgive others as Christ forgives us — with grace and compassion. Have you ever come to sacramental confession feeling like you're carrying the sin equivalent of a backpack full of rocks? And your penance is to pray one Our Father?

If we forgive others, and pray for them, we not only build stronger relationships in our work, but we can also draw ourselves closer to God, who will honor even our feeble attempts. With confession as our model, practice saying not only, "I'm sorry," to those you've offended, but also asking, "Will you please forgive me?" Then do your best to avoid similar mistakes in the future, and ask for God's grace. This all sounds familiar, right? It's just like sacramental confession . . . and the exhilarating forgiveness that results is a model for us when we forgive others.

ACTION STEPS

To grow in a spirit of forgiveness, try the following:

1. **Go to confession.** Christ is our model of forgiveness. His cry from the cross, "Father, forgive them, they know not what they do" (Luke 23:34) echoes to this very day. Receiving the grace of forgiveness helps us to grant it to others.

2. **Ask for forgiveness regularly.** Not only does this help us to grow in humility, but it also helps us to properly acknowledge our imperfections to our coworkers and rectify the hurt we cause them — and God.

3. **Grant forgiveness.** This one is tough. But the quicker we sincerely grant forgiveness, the better off we are. Lack of forgiveness causes negative emotions to fester, while granting forgiveness can heal others and always heals us. If you need inspiration, remember Rachel Muha.

4. **Make sacrifices for others.** Pray for those who wound or offend you, offer small sacrifices for them, fast for them, pray the Rosary for them. As Catholics, we know that the benefits intended for the recipients of such efforts have a happy side effect of helping us as well.

5. **Consider the upside of forgiveness.** Since we know that God's forgiveness of us is tied to our forgiveness of others, recognize the tremendous power of the small investments we make in forgiving others. It's better than a winning lottery ticket!

? QUESTIONS FOR REFLECTION

1. Have you ever experienced the need to be forgiven, or to forgive, for something serious that occurred in the workplace? How did this affect you?

2. Describe a time when asking for forgiveness helped a relationship. Are you glad that you asked?

3. Do you regularly pray for those who have wronged you in some way? Is this difficult for you?

4. Do you know anyone who seems to apologize too much? How is this different from asking for forgiveness in a way that builds interpersonal relationships?

5. Describe a time that you were wronged at work. In what ways might you make sacrifices that would help you and others involved benefit spiritually from the situation?

Chapter 12

I Love a Challenge

How to Overcome Workplace Challenges Through Perseverance

> *"For this momentary light affliction is producing for us an eternal weight of glory beyond all comparison, as we look not to what is seen but to what is unseen; for what is seen is transitory, but what is unseen is eternal."*
>
> 2 Corinthians 4:17-18

Tricycle Races

One year when planning the annual company picnic, someone had the bright idea that we should hold tricycle relay races as a competitive event. Of course, senior management was expected to participate — the thought of seeing several of us make fools of ourselves seemed to tickle the funny bone of the planning committee. The team with the best time would win less-than-lavish prizes, and a good time would be had by all.

That is, unless you happen to be 6 feet 4 inches tall, like me!

I had seen the tricycles the planning committee wanted to use. My legs didn't fit underneath the handlebars, so my attempts to propel the tricycle might be described as a hybrid of peddling and waddling. I was sure that my efforts would be not only conspicuous but thoroughly humiliating. As it turned out, I was right on both counts.

The day of the race, the weather was unexpectedly hot. Having suffered a bout of melanoma the year before, I wore long sleeves as a way of avoiding excessive sun exposure and hiding the embarrassing scar on my arm. Sweating and uncomfortable, I arrived at the starting line convinced that my team would probably lose as a direct result of my participation. As I saw my colleague Stephanie arriving with video camera in hand, my discomfort was complete.

As I anticipated, the race was over as soon as it began. Despite a concerted effort on my part, it was clearly evident that I suffered from a complete lack of talent as it pertained to tricycles. My team lost.

Now, everyone enjoys a little fun at the expense of a few members of the executive team. Previous picnics had featured a dunk tank (picture the managers in swimsuits taunting aspiring pitchers), so at least I had been spared that dishonor. But it remains a singularly memorable experience.

The Joy of Suffering . . . ?

Although appearing foolish in front of numerous coworkers was never a high priority on my list, and it wasn't much fun at the time, I was actually happy about that little tricycle race. You see, I have come to appreciate the value of humility in building relationships. Since many of our colleagues never saw the executive team outside the office, this event provided an opportunity to draw us all closer together through the great equalizer of the tricycle racetrack. After the event, I sensed a greater comfort level among the entire team — it seemed to build camaraderie and even trust.

Yet there was something else at work here. The reason I was so happy to look silly in front of others is that they truly mattered to me. It had taken many years to get to this point, and the "getting there" hadn't been easy.

Several years earlier, I had joined the company while it was on the upswing. Growth was being driven both by acquisition and organically, and we added tens of millions of dollars in revenue and hundreds of employees within a couple of years. The company was profitable, the market was hot . . . and then a disagreement erupted among the shareholders.

The next eighteen months were the most harrowing of my career. I worked excruciating hours, juggled a large number of often-conflicting priorities for different parties, and suffered through audits from every conceivable direction. My boss was fired, I wasn't sure whom I could trust, and there was a pervasive sense of fear about how this would impact us and others in the company.

It felt like the process was playing out in slow motion. Relationships were strained, with the acute uncertainty surrounding the situation, and it wasn't just business — it was personal. The character of certain executives was being subjected to scrutiny. I recall one of them, a normally stoic, strong man, being on the brink of tears one day. No one knew from day to day whether they would have a job tomorrow.

I was at the end of my rope. Perhaps you've heard the quote from Franklin D. Roosevelt: "When you come to the end of your rope, tie a knot and hang on." At the time, that was all I could do.

Biblical Wisdom

Although it may sound strange, one of my favorite Bible passages has always been Romans 5:3-5:

> . . . We even boast of our afflictions, knowing that affliction produces endurance, and endurance, proven character, and proven character, hope, and hope does not disappoint, because the love of God has been poured out into our hearts through the holy Spirit that has been given to us.

During the time when I was hanging onto the knot at the end of my rope, this theme came alive. I had been through many difficulties in life up to that point, but it became clear that *perseverance* through adversity was a key element of any worthwhile success. I also found that these difficulties became a way of relating to others who also faced trials in their lives. Suffering is so ingrained in the human experience, it can be the catalyst for unity. Through the sale process, quite unexpectedly, this is exactly what happened to the executive team.

It also became clear that perseverance through difficulties is inextricably intertwined with the virtue of hope. Consider James 1:12: "Blessed is the man who perseveres in temptation [or trial], for when he has been proved he will receive the crown of life that [God] promised to those who love him."

Now, suffering is much easier to face in the abstract. For example, would I as a husband die for my wife as Scripture teaches? Yes, of course! I can face this theoretical challenge with great imaginary valor. Yet, what if I am asked to "die to self" when it's real, by pitching in for a colleague when he or she is sick, or working on Saturday, again, when I just don't feel like it? These daily challenges aren't easy, and we often face them many times in a single day.

It's important to remember that we don't necessarily pick the challenges we face. Just like tricycle racing wasn't on my list, neither are most of the trials God allows that are meant specifically for my growth and perfection — or yours. In fact, one of the hardest parts in maintaining perspective through the tests we encounter is to recognize that they hold a divine purpose.

Making Music at Work

Now, perseverance is not only a virtue, it's also a grace. I remember a TV public-service message that reenacted the story of a child playing "Twinkle, Twinkle, Little Star" on the piano with one finger at concert hall, right before a professional recital. It didn't sound very good, until the featured pianist quietly came up behind the child, gently wrapped his arms around him, and began filling in the melody. The beautiful music that resulted brought the audience to its feet in spontaneous applause as the song ended.

In the same way, sometimes our efforts at work may be like a clunky rendition of "Twinkle, Twinkle, Little Star." But if we're willing to persevere, the Holy Spirit is like the pianist who fills in the melody and makes beautiful music despite our lack of skill.

Let's face it. We all need the help.

If we ask God to be present in our challenges, not only can He provide us with the grace to persevere, but He also can bring about the fruits of perseverance in a way that benefits both ourselves and others.

Working with others can often be an exercise in perseverance in itself. We're all unique individuals, with our own strengths and shortcomings. Yet when we use the gifts we have been given, it is like a symphony, with each person playing his or her own "instrument," or part, to make something beautiful. So whether we're in the brass section, strings, percussion (think finance, sales, operations), or when we're the conductor (CEO), our goal is identical: harmony that results in the best music we're able to bring forth.

Melanie

Sometimes relationships in the workplace are a challenge. A few years ago, I met a coworker from another office for the first time named Melanie.

Melanie was very opinionated. During our first discussion, she made numerous editorial comments on all sorts of matters, mostly painting others in a negative light. Office injustices were explained with great emotion, and she made no secret of her proposed remedies — including firing one of her coworkers! Although I remained calm externally, I was shocked at Melanie's outspoken approach.

I left the office that evening stewing. There was really nothing I liked about Melanie.

Of course, a little time and a lot of prayer have a way of changing perspectives. A week later, I had to begin working with Melanie on a project. By God's grace, I decided to hold my tongue and make the best of the situation.

Then a funny thing happened.

Through praying for Melanie, and listening more than talking, I began to see a different side of her personality. Oh, sure, she was still gruff and forthright with her opinions, but I found that there were other attributes worthy of respect, even admiration. Melanie knew her stuff. She was a hard worker, and fiercely loyal to the company. In an environment where she could have easily taken advantage of her position for personal gain, she didn't even think about it. It turns out that Melanie was a character, *with* character.

God was present in the challenge. And through His gift — in this case, a tad of well-timed humility and silence — the situation turned around completely. Grace and perseverance resulted in harmony. For the rest of my time at the company, Melanie and I worked very well together, and we developed mutual respect in the process. The relationship was harmonious.

Lessons Learned

I can't tell you how much of a lesson it was for me to just shut up. If only I could do this consistently, I would be so much better off. I'm not sure why I often feel the need to render judgment on everything (could it be that I'm a bit like Melanie?), but life seems to go better when I don't.

There was another lesson that helped in this situation, one I had learned years earlier. Simply put, it's important to be joyful and look for God in the midst of all circumstances. I kept reading Scripture passages about praying and being thankful all the time, and then one day (during a time of great trial) I was reading the Acts of the Apostles, and a passage jumped off the page at me. The story is about the apostles facing great adversity from the authorities of their day and being hauled before the Sanhedrin for preaching the Gospel:

> After recalling the apostles, they had them flogged, ordered them to stop speaking in the name of Jesus, and dismissed them. So they left the presence of the Sanhedrin, *rejoicing that they had been found worthy to suffer dishonor for the sake of the name.* (Acts 5:40-41; emphasis added)

Wow! Can you imagine? They were *beaten*, and they left rejoicing! Although this seems incredible, it hit me that day: not only are we called to rejoice and give thanks in all circumstances, we are called to look at the adversity with gratitude. God can bring good from all the situations we encounter, even from tragedy or failure. Even from being humiliated in a tricycle race, having your company sold, or working with a difficult colleague. It's a matter of placing our trust in God, even when we can't envision any positive outcome.

Now, God's timing and ours often don't coincide — we need to exercise patience along with trust. As a good friend says: Our careers aren't a sprint; they're a marathon. And just as a good runner must eat healthy food to maximize performance, so our spiritual food is the Eucharist. In terms of sacramental grace, this is the key to persevering through challenges, and to offering the Lord a fragrant offering of our best efforts.

As usual, Jesus is the ultimate example of perseverance through hardship. His model of giving Himself completely and utterly on the cross is a vivid reminder of the love we are all called to emulate. This pouring out of self, regardless of the particular challenges we are called to face, is the opportunity of our lives. The rewards are beyond words!

ACTION STEPS

To rise to the daily challenges in our work, consider the following:

1. **Sign up for a tricycle race**. Well, maybe not literally — but recognize that situations taking you out of your comfort zone may be ways to glorify God and enhance relationships with others. Humility is attractive!

2. **Never give up.** This is the answer to challenges both spiritual and practical. Perseverance is the key to overcoming obstacles of all sorts, and it is fundamentally connected to the virtue of hope. Difficulties, suffering, and bad things happening are all part of the human condition, and each one is an opportunity.

3. **Pray to the Holy Spirit.** The Holy Spirit is the key to workplace relationship harmony, along with wisdom, creativity, and excellence (among other things). Just as a pianist can help an amateur version of "Twinkle, Twinkle, Little Star" sound fantastic, so the Holy Spirit perfects our efforts, even in our weakness.

4. **Embrace adversity.** Like the apostles, develop a joyful spirit despite — and even because of — the adversity you face. Use the grace of the sacrament of the Holy Eucharist to persevere through difficulties and in love for others. Look for opportunities to pray for and help others through the everyday challenges of work.

? QUESTIONS FOR REFLECTION

1. Do you ever look at challenges as opportunities? Is it easier to do this with the benefit of hindsight? Why?

2. Do you know anyone who embraces challenges in an inspirational way? Give an example.

3. Are there any situations you are facing right now that demand prayer and perseverance? What are they?

4. Do you ever find yourself thinking about work issues in the middle of the night? What do you do when this happens?

5. When have you heard God speaking to you, through the gentle nudging of the Holy Spirit, or in other ways? How did this affect you?

Chapter 13

The Beatitudes and Business

How to Live the Beatitudes in the Workplace

> *"Blessed are the poor in spirit,*
> *for theirs is the kingdom of heaven.*
> *Blessed are they who mourn,*
> *for they will be comforted.*
> *Blessed are the meek,*
> *for they will inherit the land.*
> *Blessed are they who hunger and thirst for righteousness,*
> *for they will be satisfied.*
> *Blessed are the merciful,*
> *for they will be shown mercy.*
> *Blessed are the clean of heart,*
> *for they will see God.*
> *Blessed are the peacemakers,*
> *for they will be called children of God.*
> *Blessed are they who are persecuted for the sake of*
> *righteousness,*
> *for theirs is the kingdom of heaven.*

> *"Blessed are you when they insult you and persecute you and*
> *utter every kind of evil against you [falsely] because of me.*
> *Rejoice and be glad, for your reward will be great in heaven.*
> *Thus they persecuted the prophets who were before you."*
>
> Matthew 5:3-12

Beatitudes and Basketball

I have long enjoyed spending time with my good friend Tom. He has a great sense of humor, tells funny stories, and enjoys dishing out good-natured trash talk. He's a lot of fun to hang out with. Usually.

One day, Tom and I were at a high school basketball game. We each had a son on the team, and the guys were having a rough season. On this particular day, the boys were losing, and Tom wasn't pleased with many of the calls the refs were making: "Come on, ref! Are you blind? That was a terrible call!" Over and over, variations on this theme bellowed forth from our bleacher: "Terrible call, terrible!" I noticed the head ref glancing over in our direction several times, obviously annoyed. Then it happened.

A questionable call was made, followed by the usual howl of protest from Tom. The head ref snapped. He stopped the game, walked over to our bleacher, looked *me* squarely in the eye, and proceeded to chew me out. I sat there in stunned silence, as did Tom. When the ref was done, he turned on his heel and walked back to center court. Tom and I looked at each other in amazement, and our entire section of the bleachers — who all saw that I had been falsely accused — burst into spontaneous laughter.

Blessed Are the Persecuted?

The entire event, at least for me, wasn't so much an exercise in virtue as a demonstration of being slow witted in a completely unexpected situation. But in retrospect, I also learned something about living the beatitudes. As Matthew 5:10 says, "Blessed are they who are persecuted for the sake of righteousness, / for theirs is the kingdom of heaven." I hadn't exactly been persecuted for righteousness' sake, but being wrongly accused by the ref was valuable. It gave me a small taste, at a gut level, of how it feels to be wrongly accused.

In the workplace, these types of situations are commonplace. Shortly after this incident, one of my colleagues (a generally amiable man named Ron) sent a nasty email to another colleague by the name of Carol, expressing his contempt for her department due to a poorly handled situation that caused him to lose a client. As sometimes happens, the email was laced with emotion, and half a dozen other coworkers were copied. Ron obviously took the loss of the client personally. Unfortunately, although the situation as Ron described it was true, part of the information in the email was incorrect.

With my basketball memories fresh in my mind, and a degree of peace that only results from grace, Ron and I discussed the situation. I was careful to respect his emotions that had been triggered through the email. At the same time, I related the story of being falsely accused and described how his email had not been altogether accurate.

Whew. The Hoy Spirit was clearly in control of that meeting. After learning of his misstatements, Ron was contrite and apologized — in person — to Carol and those copied on the email. Carol, who had not jumped to her own defense right away (a workplace example of meekness, perhaps?) was vindicated, and she gained the respect of several colleagues through her gracious handling of the situation.

Of course, not all workplace conflicts are resolved so effectively, but this situation worked out well. From that point forward, Ron decided to follow the old wisdom of putting positive messages in writing and addressing negative ones in person. It was a valuable lesson.

Headaches of All Sorts

Workplace headaches like this come in many forms — and on many levels of intensity. One day, we may be falsely accused; another day we might be "downsized" out of a job and have to take a big pay cut. In our dynamic workplaces, people often lose their status, benefits, friends, money, you name it. What is a Christian to do?

Again, living the beatitudes has everything to do with our perspective. To the extent we simply regard the things that happen at work (good and bad alike) through worldly lenses, we lose an opportunity. Rather, the fully Christian outlook involves an eternal perspective. Hebrews 12:6 tells us: "For whom the Lord loves, he disciplines; / he scourges every son he acknowledges."

One of the great liberators of the beatitudes is being "poor in spirit." In its essence, this beatitude teaches us a spirit of detachment from things of this world, including those things we sometimes lose in connection with career challenges. It reminds us that we must always put God first on our priority list.

I still recall moving from a large corporate environment to a small nonprofit. Although the process was difficult at first when I considered what I had given up, I became ever more grateful as I recognized how much had been gained. Money, prestige, power, perks — the pursuit of such items pales in comparison to the pursuit of God. What I found in the new role was an extraordinary opportunity to impact others' lives for Christ. Talk about a great benefit!

Conflicts in the Computer Room

The most memorable lessons I learned about management over the years resulted from my own mistakes. Early in my years at Sony, I worked with a young woman named Beth. For the most part, we got along well. However, there was a time when I seemed to be getting on her last nerve. Beth was in her mid-twenties, and she was much more mature than I at age eighteen. So I'm sure her concerns were legitimate. But I wasn't ready for what followed.

One day, I was called into my boss's office. Rob was a good manager, known to be both smart and fair. He treated people well and had a great sense of humor. I walked in — and was immediately ill at ease. There in the chair in front of Rob's desk was Beth, looking none too pleased. "Look out!" I thought.

As it turned out, my prescient inclinations were quite correct. "Shut the door," said Rob. He then turned to Beth and nodded.

Beth fairly exploded in a torrent of negative accusations. How dare I do this, that, and the other thing! What was the matter with me, calling my college friend "dude" on the phone the other day? Why did I not demonstrate more respect for her? Did I not recognize the importance of prioritizing her requests? This type of behavior just couldn't be tolerated in a professional environment. I needed to shape up, and fast.

During Beth's diatribe, Rob sat back and somberly watched both of us. After Beth concluded her various observations and rested her case, so to speak, Rob turned to me. "Would you like to respond?"

Regrettably, my response was swift and annoyed. Beth's comments had hit some sore spots. Rather than respond directly to the allegations, I went on the attack. Why was it that Beth couldn't have handled this earlier? The fact that she went to Rob made me mad — she made lots of mistakes too! Her treatment of me had been condescending, and she had no right, given her own tendency to gossip and waste time. No one else had complained about the problems Beth identified. It was her negative personality driving the problem. By the end of my response, I was practically shaking with emotion.

After further heated discussion, Rob sat back and sighed. Amazingly, he then proceeded to give a very positive pep talk on the importance of mutual respect and the need for both of us to work together effectively. He was careful to validate both of our feelings about the situation, and he then coaxed us to recall one another's strengths. With this as a basis, he urged us to work toward a better relationship, recognizing that our mutual success was at least partly dependent on the other.

So even though I was the source of our little impromptu meeting, and didn't react well initially, I learned a few things. The relationship did improve over time, so I discovered that even intransigent relationships could be healed. Furthermore, I have often reflected on how well it was handled by Rob. In retrospect, I can understand Beth being upset — some of her concerns were well founded. I still call my college buddies "dude." Yet to this day, I am most impressed with how Rob handled the situation. Beyond good management, he demonstrated a profound respect for both Beth and me, and he played the peacemaker with aplomb.

"Blessed are the peacemakers, / for they will be called children of God" (Matthew 5:9).

Leadership: An Attitude of Beatitude

We have been given the most sublime model for living our lives as Christian disciples in the beatitudes. And of course, Jesus Himself exemplifies the beatitudes like no other.

Are we called to live the beatitudes in business? at the clinic? in the day-care center? You better believe it! Remember, holiness is about allowing the faith to permeate *every* aspect of our lives, including our daily work. I can't imagine Jesus ever telling us that we need to check our faith at the door during work hours.

So can you be meek when you have a sales quota to hit? Yes! Can you be merciful when human resources demands you treat everyone the same? Yes! Are you better off for having been persecuted? By God's grace, yes.

Applying our faith in the workplace shouldn't hold us back from achieving our practical goals at work — it should help! Although Jesus was the model of meekness, His human accomplishments were extraordinary. Tradition tells us He excelled as a carpenter, and think of the "success" of His public ministry. It's incredible.

Leadership, in its very essence, is the imitation of Jesus Christ. In our work. In our home. In our school. In our family. Everywhere we go, we are called to follow, imitate, and persevere until our very lives are poured out fully, thereby returning all our gifts to God.

Think of the strong-willed coworker who is adamant about seeing justice done for their customer who has been through a bad experience with your company. He may say something like: "I don't care what our policy is on returning merchandise; we need to make this situation right!" and walk away with fierce determination, focused on a goal. Leadership always hungers and thirsts for righteousness, sometimes even when it costs money in the short term. Money isn't the highest value — although paradoxically, through great service, financial goals are often met in the long run. God Himself is our final destination, our hope, our facilitator — and He must be our greatest (and only) ultimate goal.

As a result, the beatitudes are the roadmap to true leadership. The beatitudes instruct us about detachment, and they instruct us about love of others and of God. If we are properly detached from the world, from sin, and from self-love, we are able to focus on others and serve them. If we seek to love and serve God first, and others as ourselves, how can we go wrong?

Good Mourning

In today's workplaces, there are many who mourn. Perhaps it's a lost job, a lost culture through the acquisition of another company, a lost election, even a child lost to college for a full-time mom! In our walk with Christ, we can always look forward.

The emotions in difficult situations are real, but so is our hope in Jesus. We can always trust in His plan.

I know a number of close friends who have mourned the loss of a job in recent years. One former colleague, Mark, found this particularly difficult since it impacted his sense of self-worth as a husband and a father. He also experienced feelings of worthlessness and insecurity as he sought another position and was turned down over and over again.

Yet through this process, Mark was forced to reexamine his priorities. Through prayer and research — as well as conversations with his wife, spiritual adviser, and trusted friends — he decided to make a career change. Rather than going back into human resources, he started up his own company and became a recruiter, working with several organizations. Although he gave up the predictability of a regular paycheck, he is actually better off financially and finds that he has more time to spend with his wife and children. At first, he mourned, but true to the beatitude, he has been comforted.

It's All About Execution

In order to make this a reality, we must *execute*. So what's the secret?

It's simple. *Be a good Catholic!*

Believe everything the Church teaches. Embrace the sacraments, those holy and beautiful gifts God has given us. (You wouldn't refuse a gift from such a loving God, would you?) Read and cherish the Scriptures. Pray like your life depends on it — because it does. Pray the Rosary. Ask for saintly intercession. Be part of the faith community. Love others, even those with whom you disagree. Work with purpose. And never give up!

Then begin again tomorrow, and do it all over, until your tomorrows run out.

Everyone can live the beatitudes at work. Lead others to Jesus and to His Church by living the faith we share, and even by using words. If others choose not to follow, lead anyway.

I am convinced that if we could even vaguely wrap our minds around the brevity of our lives relative to eternity, we would spend every second trying to draw closer to God. Our work is an *essential* part of our holy calling as Christians: we were meant to work, and in doing so, we have a beautiful opportunity to lift up our efforts to the Lord. In sanctifying every second of our workday, we accomplish our life's purpose and make ordinary events extraordinary, and natural outcomes supernatural.

Hope Springs Eternal

My hope for you, my prayer and my desire, is that you be so caught up in love for our Lord that you dedicate the rest of your life — including your work life — to working for Him. Don't just work for a paycheck. Do your *postmortem* retirement planning. It's not just tax-deferred — it's tax-free!

Your career really can help you become a saint. An eternity of joy awaits. Be there!

ACTION STEPS

To live the beatitudes in your work, pray about the following, and spend the rest of your life perfecting your execution:

1. **Be poor in spirit**. Poverty in spirit begins with detachment from worldly concerns. It's a great place to start, as work provides a tremendous opportunity to find purpose, serve humanity, and glorify God.

2. **Pour yourself out for others**. There is a particular grace associated with taking "hits" for others, whether it's at a

basketball game or at work. Even under the most agoniz-
ing circumstances, conduct yourself honorably. If you are
falsely accused, or wronged in another way, count it all joy.

3. **Be a peacemaker.** Graces abound for those who put themselves in harm's way to act as peacemakers. This takes courage, but even our most timid efforts can be blessed in
unforeseen ways. Pray for those who persecute you, and for
others for the sake of peace.

4. **Be a good Catholic.** We are so blessed to have the tools
to live sacramental lives. Embrace the sacraments to their
fullest — they're designed specifically for our benefit! If
it's impossible to be a good Catholic in your job, you're in
the wrong place.

QUESTIONS FOR REFLECTION

1. Do you know anyone who is a model of the beatitudes in
your workplace? Give an example of a time you saw this in
action.

2. Were you ever falsely accused? How did it make you feel?

3. Have you ever seen difficult situations turn around and
become positive in the long run? What happened?

4. Are there any people in your workplace who excel as peacemakers? How does this affect your workplace's culture?

5. List three things you will do as a result of reading this book
that will change the way you approach your work in the
future.

Take a Break!

"Come away by yourselves to a deserted place and rest a while."
Mark 6:31

It's important to consider the opportunities of living our faith, and of finding the purpose of our work beyond the paycheck. So important, in fact, that we might need a bit of time for reflection.

Have you ever spent ridiculous hours trying to accomplish a task, working so hard that you seem to lose perspective? In the end, we're just not engineered to work all the time. It's important to sanctify our work; it's also important that we don't let our work take over our lives.

I recently ran into this problem. I was crazy busy, trying to accomplish multiple tasks, tired, cranky, and pretty much just worn out. At home one evening, my youngest daughter said: "Daddy, will you play with me?"

What happened that evening defies business logic. We had a tea party with some of her stuffed animals. It was hard to slow down, but it was the best thing I did all day. Interestingly, the following day was far more productive.

We all need to find some quiet in our daily lives, often characterized by a relentless pace and unprecedented accessibility. So here's my final bit of encouragement to you: take time to recharge your batteries, probably just as often as you recharge your cell phone. Here are just a couple of ideas.

- Set aside quiet prayer time every day.
- Be silent before the Eucharist regularly.
- Take a *real* vacation or long weekend.
- Make an annual retreat.
- Take time to think, talk, and dream.

Give thanks to God for the gifts He has given each of us, for *He is the purpose of our work*. May God bless you!

About the Author

Kevin Lowry is a writer and speaker on topics including faith, work, finances, and conversion. He spent twenty years in secular financial and executive-management roles, and he currently serves as chief operating officer of The Coming Home Network International. Kevin and his wife, Kathi, are converts to the Catholic faith and have eight children. Kevin blogs at gratefulconvert.com.